RESILIENCE
AND PERSONAL
EFFECTIVENESS
FOR SOCIAL WORKERS

RESILIENCE
AND PERSONAL
EFFECTIVENESS
FOR SOCIAL WORKERS

— JIM GREER —

Los Angeles | London | New Delhi
Singapore | Washington DC | Melbourne

Los Angeles | London | New Delhi
Singapore | Washington DC | Melbourne

SAGE Publications Ltd
1 Oliver's Yard
55 City Road
London EC1Y 1SP

SAGE Publications Inc.
2455 Teller Road
Thousand Oaks, California 91320

SAGE Publications India Pvt Ltd
B 1/I 1 Mohan Cooperative Industrial Area
Mathura Road A
New Delhi 110 044

SAGE Publications Asia-Pacific Pte Ltd
3 Church Street
#10-04 Samsung Hub
Singapore 049483

Editor: Kate Wharton
Editorial assistant: Lucy Dang
Production editor: Katie Forsythe
Copyeditor: Clare Weaver
Proofreader: William Baginsky
Indexer: Silvia Benvenuto
Marketing manager: Camille Richmond
Cover design: Lisa Harper-Wells
Typeset by: C&M Digitals (P) Ltd, Chennai, India
Printed and bound by Ashford Colour Press Ltd,
Gosport, Hampshire

At SAGE we take sustainability seriously. Most of our
products are printed in the UK using FSC papers and
boards. When we print overseas we ensure sustainable
papers are used as measured by the PREPS grading
system. We undertake an annual audit to monitor our
sustainability.

Library of Congress Control Number: 2015960260

British Library Cataloguing in Publication data

A catalogue record for this book is available from
the British Library

ISBN 978-1-4739-1916-7
ISBN 978-1-4739-1917-4 (pbk)

At SAGE we take sustainability seriously. Most of our products are printed in the UK using FSC papers and boards.
When we print overseas we ensure sustainable papers are used as measured by the PREPS grading system.
We undertake an annual audit to monitor our sustainability.

To my wife Liz: Who has accompanied me on my whole social work journey and had a key role in starting it. Thank you!

CONTENTS

ABOUT THE AUTHOR

Jim Greer left a career in local government auditing to become a volunteer on Community Service Volunteer's Independent Living Scheme, an invaluable experience which gave him insight into the lived experience of service users and the reality of being a full time carer. Since qualifying Jim worked initially as a generic social worker, before specialising in adult mental health and subsequently being promoted to Team Manager. More recently Jim worked as a Project Manager for a Regional Improvement and Efficiency Partnership, responsible for a number of projects which applied new technologies in social care.

Jim has also taught psychology, social care and social work for a number of years, sometimes in parallel with other roles. He is currently Principal Lecturer in Social Work, Teesside University. He is a member of the British Psychological Society and promotes the value of psychological and scientific approaches in social work education. He also utilises his experience in finance and service improvement in the teaching of organisational issues. He combines his academic duties with other roles including social work course endorsement and being a standing member of a committee of the National Institute for Health and Care Excellence.

PREFACE

During the period in which this was being written there has been an increasing focus on the importance of resilience in social work and other professions in health and social care, including workshops at conferences and online seminars. This is partly as a result of the high staff turnover rates in these professions and partly as a result of the growing awareness of the additional stresses which cuts have placed on public services and those who work in them.

The ambition of this book is to provide guidance to social workers not only in dealing with the impact of stressors in the workplace but also in managing the sources of stress. The book has a highly practical focus and, to get the most from it, readers should set aside time to do the reflective exercises contained in each chapter. No amount of reading or resolve is going to help change how we cope with work unless it is backed up by action. Unproductive and unhelpful work habits are hard to break and new approaches can only become established behaviours with conscious repetition and perseverance. I would recommend keeping a journal to record progress which you make in achieving change in your relationship with work and your ability to cope with it.

The book is structured in a way which will enable workers to evaluate their own relationship with work before looking at how they can develop practical strategies to make their work more productive and less stressful.

The first three chapters of the book are all about the direct physical and psychological impact of stressors. The first chapter begins with a guide to identifying the signs of stress and burnout and the consequences for one's health and wellbeing. The second chapter moves on to define resilience and why it is important for social workers and the third chapter considers how social workers can achieve a satisfactory work/life balance. The emphasis in all three chapters is on the reader exploring for themselves what constitutes resilience and an ideal work/life balance. Wellbeing has different meanings for different people and work has a different role and a different degree of importance in each person's life. For these reasons each reader has top find their own answers about how they achieve balance and harmony in their lives. The interactive approach of the chapters is designed to help each reader to explore these issues and come up with answers and strategies which meet their objectives and are achievable for them.

Chapters 4 and 5 move the focus away from wellbeing and towards personal effectiveness. Readers will be helped to make better use of time and make maximum use of the capabilities of new technology. Effective use of time can reduce the likelihood of having to take work home and free up time for meaningful interaction with service users and other elements of the job which social workers find satisfying.

Chapters 6, 7 and 8 explore the interpersonal aspects of effective and fulfilling social work practice. Chapter 6 highlights the fact that managers and co-workers can sometimes be sources of stress. Social workers normally enter the profession with a positive view about the integrity and values of their colleagues. However, bullying, discrimination and conflict occur in social work just as they do in other professions and this chapter considers how workers can deal with interpersonal problems in the workplace. Chapter 7 considers how good quality reflective supervision is essential to social work and looks at the roles of social workers and their supervisors in maximising the benefits of supervision. Chapter 8 explores the relationship between managers and their staff and how to be a good leader and a good follower. The chapter also looks at the role of effective management and good leadership in creating a healthy and productive workplace where staff feel valued and supported.

The final chapter sets out how social workers can manage their career over the long term to ensure that it meets their goals while achieving positive outcomes for the people they work with.

The book is informed by psychological ideas ancient and modern. There is a growing rediscovery and appreciation of the Buddhist mindfulness by modern psychologists and therapists. There is also a reappraisal of ancient philosophical traditions such as stoicism by modern management writers. Parallel to this, concepts such as lean management, which comes from the automotive industry are being successfully applied to human services. This book applies ideas from a range of traditions in therapy, psychology, philosophy and management in a way which is compatible with the values of social work and the realities of modern social work practice.

I hope you find this book readable, informative and helpful and value your feedback.

1

STRESS AND THE SOCIAL WORK ROLE

Key Concepts and Issues in this Chapter

- The importance of resilience for social workers
- The centrality of emotional labour in social work
- Impact of the political and economic climate and the media on social work
- Physical and psychological effects of stress
- Understanding the nature of burnout
- How to understand when we are stressed or experiencing burnout
- Internal and external loci of control and how they affect our response to stress
- Practical steps to develop an internal locus of control

Why resilience is important in social work

If you were lucky enough to have a foreign holiday this year you will have (or should have) listened to a cabin safety announcement. One of the things about the safety announcement which is memorable to me and which relates to my decision to write this book is the set of instructions for using oxygen masks. The announcement tells you to fit your own oxygen mask before you fit your child's mask or help anyone else with theirs. Our first instinct would of course be to help our child or someone else who appeared to be having problems and so the advice goes contrary to what our natural response might be in an emergency. There is, however, a good reason for putting our own mask on first. We can only help another person when we are able to breathe properly ourselves. Far from being selfish, the action of securing our own oxygen supply first is essential to us being able to help others. I first heard this analogy on a podcast by the business blogger James Altucher. It came back to me a year ago when I was interviewed as part of a research study on resilience and social work education. I was asked in the telephone interview why I thought it was important for social workers to be resilient and I used the oxygen mask example as a way of explaining why we cannot help others effectively without also caring for ourselves.

Resilience is the quality which all social workers need for the emotionally demanding tasks of the job. Soldiering on when we are burnt out and drained may sound noble, but to be an effective and safe practitioner we need to be able to think clearly and retain our capacity for empathy and warmth.

At its most extreme, the inability to cope with the emotional demands of social work can lead to **burnout** which means a complete inability to engage effectively with one's colleagues and service users. Pines and Maslach (1978) described burnout as involving a negative self-concept, negative job attitudes and a loss of concern and feeling for clients. In a profession where the relationship with service users is central, burnout involves a fundamental inability to practise effectively or safely.

Farber (1983) notes that burnout has individual, organisational and societal factors. Clearly it is individual factors which you as a social work student or first line practitioner have most control over so this book will focus on advice on how you can look after your own wellbeing. However, as social workers we also have responsibilities to our colleagues and there are some stressors which are due to organisational factors so the book will also look at mechanisms for collective responses to workplace stress.

Social work as emotional labour

Social work does not usually involve physical heavy lifting. We are unlikely to develop a bad back or physical strain from the job – other than perhaps the strain of leaning over a computer writing case notes. However, social work does involve psychological heavy lifting. Arlie Hochschild (1983), a sociologist, developed the concept of emotional labour to describe the emotional demands involved in human services professions (an American term covering social work, occupational therapy, etc.). Emotional labour involves having to manage the outward expression of our emotions. As social workers we have to show empathy and concern even when we are exhausted and have little left to give. We have to be able to give our full attention and focus to the problems of others even when we are preoccupied with problems of our own. Elements of the problems of others may conjure up unsettling feelings about our own personal relationships (past or present), memories of previous losses or bereavements or even unhappy events from our childhood. When this happens we have to put these feelings aside and continue to focus on the service user. We also have to suppress anger we might feel about service users' behaviours towards others or irritation we might feel about their inability to change their situation. We have to project a professional persona in the face of demands, aggression, threats or even violence from service users, their relatives or others in the community. We must be non-judgemental when service users make life choices which we disagree with and yet express genuine joy when they achieve positive change. We must sometimes implement laws and policies, which on a personal level we feel are unfair, and yet we often cannot share our feelings about this with colleagues or service users. Having one's emotions on show constantly means having to suppress some feelings (when they are negative) and bring others to the fore when we have to show empathy or support. This involves a great deal of self-regulation. This is emotional labour and it is one of the most stressful elements of the social work task.

An added dimension is that emotional labour in social work involves dealing with problems which are chronic and entrenched (such as poverty) or which involve high likelihood of relapse (such as substance misuse). This can lead to disappointment and frustration for social workers who invest a great deal emotionally in their work. I have heard social workers tell me that they have taken two generations of children into care from the same family. Such experiences are dispiriting and can lead to workers questioning the validity of their work.

Exercise

Emotional Labour

Think of a work situation which had a significant negative emotional impact on you (though not something which was a major trauma or tragedy). What feelings did you have and how did they impact on how you felt for the rest of the day or week? Did the incident or event spill over into your time outside work? Did you get support from colleagues or your line manager? When you think about the event does it bring up powerful feelings again? Do you experience any physical feelings such as tension in your face

(Continued)

(Continued)

or body or a change in posture? If you tensed up physically then try to relax the muscles which became tense. Breathe slowly and deeply until you feel some of the tension dissipate.

Now think of an incident or event which gave you positive feelings such as hope or happiness. Think about the impact of this event and again try to get in touch with changes in your mood and any physical changes in your body.

What does thinking about these experiences tell you about how you react emotionally and physically to the emotional labour of social work?

External sources of stress for social work

In addition to the stresses which are inherent in the social work task, there are a number of other sources of stress which have put additional psychological pressures on social workers over the past decade.

Austerity

The global financial crisis of 2008 led to austerity policies across the USA and Europe to reduce government deficits, which involved the cutting and scaling back of public services. In Greece and Portugal this was particularly severe as swingeing public spending cutbacks were a requirement for sovereign bailouts. In the UK austerity cuts were a prominent policy of the Conservative/Liberal Democrat Coalition Government which came to power in 2010 and have been continued by the Conservative Government following their 2015 general election victory; and they seem to be set to continue at least for the rest of the decade. Furthermore, the fact that certain categories of public expenditure such as the health service have been protected from cuts has meant that the unprotected areas such as social care spending have been disproportionately affected.

Squeezed social services budgets have led to less resources for dealing with social problems and fewer opportunities for preventative work. This creates pressures and professional dilemmas for social workers who cannot provide the sorts of interventions for their service users which they feel are needed.

A survey of social work professionals conducted by the British Association of Social Workers (2012) found that 88 per cent of respondents believed that lives could be put at risk by cuts to services and 77 per cent considered their caseloads to be unmanageable.

A report by the Local Government Association found that between 2010/11 and 2013/14 local authorities had achieved savings of £10 billion through finding efficiencies but that budgets will have fallen in real terms by 33 per cent in the period to 2019/20. It is difficult to continue to cut budgets at those sorts of rates in the face of increasing demands on services without seriously affecting essential services.

The situation in local authorities is mirrored by uncertainty and instability in the voluntary sector. A report by the National Council for Voluntary Organisations (2013) found that while new sources of funding such as payment by results were emerging, voluntary sector organisations were struggling to secure the finance which they needed. The report predicted that in 2017/18, voluntary sector funding was likely to be £1.7 billion lower than it was in 2010/11 (at 2010/11 prices). Furthermore, the replacement of block grants to the voluntary sector with bidding for contracts has further reduced the stability of funding in that sector and instruments such as social impact bonds seem likely to cause further instability and uncertainty.

Austerity has also had an impact on the earnings of social workers through wage freezes and below inflation increases across the term of the Coalition Government and subsequent Conservative Governments. Social workers, in common with other public sector workers, face threats of the removal of automatic pay progression, traditionally a reward for experience and level of responsibility. These cuts add personal financial woes to the other forms of stress which austerity has brought to social workers. They also contribute to public sector workers feeling that what they do is not being valued.

Social workers also experience anger and frustration about the impact of austerity policies on the most vulnerable in society. In a later chapter there will be some suggestions about how these feelings can be positively channelled.

Outsourcing and other changes to how social services are organised

In business, outsourcing is a commonly used method of accessing specialised expertise in a flexible and efficient way. However, outsourcing in public services has in many cases been principally a way of reducing labour costs. Cutting the pay of existing employees would be politically sensitive but by transferring the employees to the private sector, the unpleasant task of cutting workers' pay and conditions is privatised along with the work. This weakens transparency and reduces the opportunities for trade unions to monitor and safeguard the conditions of employees. A report by The Adam Smith Institute (2014), commissioned by the public sector union Unison, found that 'huge public-sector cuts are determining the objectives, nature and outcomes of the latest outsourcing deals' and that reducing costs was the 'key objective' of outsourcing.

So far, it has been the jobs of lower paid care staff which have been outsourced but there has recently been a bill (Deregulation Bill) to allow the outsourcing of qualified social work jobs. This may lead to social workers setting themselves up in small practices and there are some potential benefits to this model in terms of professional independence. However, fears about social work being transferred to unpopular private companies with poor reputations led a number of senior practitioners and academics to write a letter of concern to the *Guardian* on 16 May 2014.

Outsourcing, regardless of any potential benefits to social workers who form independent practices, contributes to a climate of uncertainty and disquiet amongst social workers.

Media scrutiny and criticism of social work

There is a widespread belief amongst social workers that there is a strong media bias against the profession. Some evidence for this view was provided by a study by *Community Care* (2009) of newspaper coverage of social work issues during a three-month period. This study found a disproportionate amount of negative media coverage of social work and social workers. Greer (2014) suggested that local authorities need to be more open and proactive in engaging with the media and should allow social workers to speak directly to the press. It is difficult to blame the media for one-sided coverage when our own side does not comment.

However, regardless of why media bias occurs, it is demoralising for the social worker to see their profession regularly being the focus of negative media attention.

New public management

Harris (2007) described the changes that have taken place in human services management in the UK and USA since the 1980s as a move away from traditional administrative management (with an underlying respect for professionalism) to a transformational approach, which borrows heavily from management in the commercial world. He identified this approach as underlying a number of trends: contracting (including purchaser/provider split); consumerism; performance indicators (working to targets); getting more for less; increased scrutiny (including use of standardised assessment tools, eligibility criteria, etc.); and gate keeping and rationing.

Harris (2007: 20) suggests that there has been a more nuanced approach in adopting new public management in the USA where 'social welfare management' is seen as requiring its own special set of knowledge and skills. By contrast, UK professionals are more likely to be faced with the imposition of a more generic model of management which assumes that the public sector constantly needs to look to the private sector for inspiration. This unsubtle approach breeds resentment about deprofessionalisation and gets in the way of dialogue between the social work profession and politicians. Harris (2003) explained how a 'business discourse' within social work has arisen as part of a wider colonisation of the public services by the 'culture of capitalism'. Since then the trends which Harris identified have continued and seem certain to carry on.

Eileen Munro (2011), in her review of child protection services, said that a focus on rules and regulations reduced the time available for social workers to carry out their assessments and that a target-driven culture has reduced the scope for professional judgement.

There are countless articles and books which express derogatory views about changes in public sector management with very vitriolic views on managerialism and neoliberalism. Frequently, this critique is applied as much to approaches which have the potential for reducing bureaucracy as it is to the procedures which increase it. Within the social work literature all forms of service improvement are often seen as undermining professionalism. For example, Ferguson (2008) in the introduction to his book *Reclaiming Social Work*, lampoons an advertisement for a course on the service improvement model known as Lean management.

Whether the commentary of Ferguson and others is fair or not, new public management presents a problem for social work because of the degree of resentment it provokes between the profession and politicians and the general negativity which it seems to generate in the social work academic press. This must inevitably contribute to a general feeling within the profession that it is under attack.

New technology and changes in approaches to working

Technology has changed the way people work a great deal. The traditional model of working 9 to 5 in an office has changed to a much more flexible set of options including working from home, hot desking, and answering emails in the evening or at weekends. While these changes have increased opportunities to work flexibly they have also had other less desirable effects. The ability to work from home has blurred the demarcation between work and home life causing people to work at times when they should be relaxing or spending time with their family. Even holidays are no longer sacred with some organisations expecting managers to answer their emails or even phone calls when they are on holiday with their families.

McGregor (2012a) reported a survey which found that 9 out of 10 social workers believed that hot desking on social services damaged worker morale and increased their stress.

Recording data and case notes on computer systems is another area of concern which is claimed to be a frequent source of stress. In another report McGregor (2012b) stated that social workers were 'drowning in admin'. Smith (2012) gave a first-hand report from a child protection social worker who claimed that the ICS recording system was the 'bane of his life'. Other social workers report a feeling of loss about the camaraderie of an office environment and the opportunities it gives for seeking advice from more experienced colleagues.

In theory, new technology should be making people's lives easier, in addition to making them more productive. Even hot desking can have significant benefits if implemented properly and adequately resourced. Clearly, the amount of dissatisfaction which social workers experience suggests that either the technology is not being used correctly or that it is inadequate to the needs of social workers. I will discuss in a later chapter how you can use technology to your benefit and how managers can help their staff to use technology effectively. This is, however, one area which requires investment and forethought at an organisational level. Technology is not a panacea and changes in working practices should not be seen solely as ways to save money. Abolishing permanent offices with desks for individuals is a way of saving money, but there needs to be thought given to replacing the functions of an office including opportunities for exchanging knowledge with colleagues. At present, we can say that there is evidence that new technology is a source of stress for a significant number of social workers.

Physical and psychological effects of stress

With all the stressors discussed in the previous section it is no wonder that the sector as a whole is experiencing a great deal of strain and tension. Stress can adversely affect the culture and working environment of an organisation and we will look at the implications of this for managers in a later chapter. For now, however, we will focus on the effects of stress at an individual level.

Traditionally in Western medicine we have diagnosed and treated physical and mental ill health separately. However, as more is becoming understood about the relationship between psychological stress and physical wellbeing a more balanced model is developing which acknowledges that mind and body are very closely linked. This is one of the reasons that many people turn for help to alternative therapies. Despite the view of the established medical profession that most alternative therapies lack an evidence base, many people enjoy the holistic approach that they receive from a holistic therapist.

Any serious or chronic physical health will have a psychological impact, and serious or chronic psychological problems can impact on our physical health. If we are getting enough rest and sleep then we are less likely to contract infections. Conversely, if we are lacking sleep through stress or anxiety then our resistance to infections will be reduced. Good physical health will help us to deal with psychological stressors in the workplace and home life whereas an ongoing physical health problem leaves us with less capacity to deal with these stressors.

Classic studies in the relationship between stress and general health

Selye (1956) came up with a model of how the body responded to stress. He said that the stress response consisted of three phases: **alarm phase, resistance phase and exhaustion phase.**

The **alarm phase** is what is popularly known as the flight or fight response. It involves preparing the body for action to deal with an immediate threat. The hypothalamus sends messages to the pituitary gland which causes the release of hormones which in turn cause the release of adrenaline and other hormones. One of the effects is to increase respiration and heart rate. This is to ensure that tissues are oxygenated to allow the body to respond to the demands of running away from danger or fighting an adversary or predator. There is also a release of cholesterol and fat into the blood to act as an energy source. Blood is also diverted from the skin to the brain and the muscles, where it is needed for dealing with the threat. Blood pressure increases and the blood becomes more coagulated to help deal with injuries in the event of the body being cut or otherwise injured.

As you can imagine this is a very useful set of physiological responses if you are having to run away from a bear or take part in a gladiatorial fight in the arena in ancient Rome. However, it is a poor response for most of the stressors which we face in today's society. If someone cuts in on us when we are in a queue for a petrol pump we may feel a strong sense of territorialism as a result of them stealing 'our pump'. However, the laws and conventions of our society prevent us from storming into action and assaulting our rival. Even if we say something to the other person or sound our horn we will not be indulging in the sort of physical activity which our body is primed for. If we have the sort of personality which has strong and frequent reactions to such incursions by other people then we may be getting very angry several times per day. If we have an unhappy work environment in which we feel that other people are not pulling their weight or are deliberately trying to outdo us or cause us mischief then we may have ongoing feelings of resentment which intermittently give rise to anger.

These feelings of anger and resentment can be very damaging to our physical health. The fats which are released into our bloodstream as part of the flight or flight response will, if not used through energetic activity, continue to linger in the bloodstream where they can block our arteries. These blockages can in turn raise our blood pressure (hypertension).

The second stage in Selye's model is the **resistance** phase. This is where the body returns to a normal state of arousal and any tissues which have been damaged are repaired.

However, if the body fails to go into the resistance phase because of chronic stress or over-work the result is **exhaustion**. The body has been unable to effectively repair itself and as a result we are more likely to fall victim to a stress-related illness.

Another negative effect of chronic stressors is learned helplessness. This phenomenon was discovered by Seligman (1975). Through a series of (somewhat cruel) animal experiments, Seligman found that if an animal comes to learn that it cannot avoid electric shocks through its own actions it will eventually stop trying and will become withdrawn and apathetic. The animal has learned that there is no contingency between its responses to an unpleasant situation and the outcome. This is called learned helplessness. Seligman proposed that a similar process might contribute to the development of depression in humans. If we are faced with a number of serious setbacks within a short space of time we may begin to give up trying to improve our situation. The result is a descent into despair and depression. It is easy to see how experiences of impossible caseloads, constant demands and bureaucratic management culture can wear some staff down to the extent that they believe that they can never get on top of their work. As a result they cease to get any enjoyment from working.

Burnout

When work-related stress becomes chronic and its effects become profound then it can manifest in a condition known as burnout. Farber (1983) noted that burnout consists of attitudinal, emotional and physical components. Pines and Aronson (1981) stated that burnout was 'characterised by physical depletion, by feelings of helplessness and hopelessness, by emotional drain, by the development of negative self-concept and negative attitudes towards work, life and other people'. They further stated that burnout is a 'sense of distress, discontent and failure in the quest for ideals'. It is easy to see how this state would lead to damage to one's home life and personal relationships. It will also lead to poor work performance, poor judgement and callousness. Maslach (1976) said that burned-out professionals 'lose all concern, all emotional feelings for the persons they work with and come to treat them in detached or even dehumanised ways'. This is in fact what appears to happen in cases where people who need care and support are ignored, neglected or mistreated by those who should be responsible for their care. Burnout therefore has very serious personal and professional implications and can result in very serious deviations from good practice. Burnout can also ruin careers and lead to skilled and experienced staff leaving the workforce. Identifying burnout is therefore an important task for individuals and organisations.

Farber (1983) notes that Cherniss (1980a and 1980b) identified that public sector professionals coming into service have unrealistic views about how much professional autonomy and job satisfaction they will have and that they therefore become very disillusioned and burned out when they experience the reality of working in large bureaucracies. This would seem to fit with the reports on sites such as *Community Care* which regularly report newly qualified workers quickly becoming disillusioned and wanting to leave the profession. In light of this it may be important for educators and employers to better manage staff expectations of what their experience of work will be. It is also essential that we help social workers to manage their stress, build up strategies to protect themselves and be aware of when they or any of their colleagues are showing the symptoms of stress or burnout.

How stress manifests itself

The way in which symptoms of stress are manifested varies between individuals and there are differences between different groups. Men, for example, are more likely than women to turn to drugs or alcohol as a result of mental distress. There are also differences between cultures and societies. For example, susto is a condition which involves anxiety, insomnia and panic symptoms and is only reported in certain Latin American cultures (Castillo, 1997). It shares some of the symptoms of mental disorders commonly described in European societies but the combination of symptoms and the beliefs about the causes are culturally bound. People from all cultures experience mental distress but the way in which it is experienced appears to be culturally mediated. The cultural nature of mental illness needs to be borne in mind when listening to people from cultural groups other than our own. People may have different ways of describing mental distress and it is best not to make assumptions about what someone means when they are describing how they feel.

Racism is an additional factor which can add to the stresses facing people from ethnic minorities. Sadly, health and social care workplaces are not always free from racism and other forms of discrimination.

An individual's previous experience of mental distress can also affect how mental distress is expressed. For example, people with a previous history of obsessive compulsive behaviours, substance misuse problems or anxiety may suffer a relapse or a worsening of symptoms as a result of stress at work.

Recognising we are stressed

The following is a list of possible symptoms which could indicate that a person is stressed. Any amount of these can be present in any combination. It is important to note that a number of these symptoms could also be an indication of a serious health problem and that you should always consult your doctor about any health worries which you have.

Possible symptoms of stress:

- Insomnia
- Sleeping much more than normal
- Tearfulness
- Mood swings
- Inability to enjoy life or get pleasure from things we would normally enjoy
- Low libido or sexual dysfunction
- Problems concentrating or remembering things
- Impatience, anger or irritation
- Loss of appetite
- Compulsive eating or other excessive patterns of consumption or spending
- Bitterness or resentment towards others
- Feelings of failure
- Headaches, muscular aches and tension in body or face and muscular tics
- Inability to relax
- Lack of attention possibly leading to accidents or mistakes
- Feelings of helplessness or hopelessness
- Inability to be focused or productive at work
- Recklessness
- Inability to make decisions
- Worsening or relapse of skin problems such psoriasis
- Excessive stress and conflict in relationships with family, friends or colleagues
- Lack of patience or empathy with service users

This is only a partial list and it might be just as valid to say any significant change in behaviour or temperament. It is not always possible for people who are suffering from stress to recognise that their mood or their ability to cope has changed. Sometimes it requires a friend, colleague or manager to point out that someone seems to be speaking or behaving out of character. This can be difficult as a person who is extremely stressed can become very fixed in their belief that they have to press on and accomplish the impossible goals which they have set themselves. The idea that they should rest and relax can itself be seen initially by them as an additional pressure.

An important skill for social workers to develop is an ability to be able to recognise when their own thoughts, behaviours or relationships with others are different from normal. What is fundamentally important, however, is to have a good baseline work/life balance. If we normally have a good approach to eating, sleeping, exercising and socialising then this will make it easier when we have to deal with periods of exceptional stress or demands from work or family.

Individual differences in how we personally deal with threats to our wellbeing

The earlier section in this chapter about the stresses on social workers may have given the impression that social work is always a highly stressful and emotionally draining job which is not valued by wider society and is under constant attack from media and politicians. One might wonder why then there are so many social workers who are still committed to their job and would not want to do any other kind of work. When I visit students on placement I am constantly impressed by just how much high quality work and innovative practice is being done in social work settings.

For many people, a certain amount of stress is a challenge and a source of motivation. One factor which affects how we deal with sources of threat is our own sense of volition. Do we feel we are in control of what happens to us or are we dependent on the actions of others?

Rotter (1966) introduced the concept of **locus of control**. Locus of control refers to the degree to which we think we are personally responsible for achieving positive change in our life. If we have an internal locus of control we think that the success or failure we experience in our life is down to our own efforts. An external locus of control means that we think that chance, fate and external forces are mainly responsible for what happens to us. An internal locus of control is thought be more beneficial in a number of areas of life. For example, if we believe that we are responsible for our own health we are more likely to eat sensibly and exercise. If we believe that our health is mainly determined by our genes or is down to luck then we are less likely to engage in behaviours which will benefit our health. Thus, an internal locus of control is likely to be linked to more positive health outcomes. This holds regardless of just how much control individuals have over their health as people who look after themselves will always have better health than if they had not done so. In terms of our more general well-being, an internal locus of control will lead to us taking more responsibility for all elements of our lives and make it more likely that we will perform behaviours which are beneficial to us.

Thinking about why we might have an internal or external locus of control

As we develop through life, our experiences influence how we understand the world. We develop a model of the world and how we interact with it. Beck et al. (1979) referred to these internal mental structures as schemata. Schemata help us to make predictions about what is going to happen in a given situation and how we are supposed to behave and what to do. For example, I have a schema about myself in relation to DIY. I think that I am impractical and poorly co-ordinated and so my efforts at DIY are likely to end in disaster. Thus if I had to have a major home improvement project to do then I would hire someone to do it for me. My schema about this is partly based on genuine experience of having tried to do DIY in the past and getting it horribly wrong. However, it is also based on a more general lack of confidence about practical things and a lack of positive experience from having given up too easily in the past. There are circumstances in which my schema about DIY might change. If a friend who was good at DIY mentored me through a small home improvement project I might discover that with help I was actually capable of doing a reasonable job. Having a small success in this area might change my beliefs about myself. My internal psychological model about myself might be changed and I might become motivated to try further home improvement projects, which, if success-ful, would further improve my confidence and further change my mental model about my abilities.

Our locus of control can be thought of as a generalised schema or mental model about ourselves in relation to the world. It will influence the response we make to a range of situations. It is something which can change as a result of our experiences. Through practice we can develop a more positive sense of our own abilities and the power we have to shape our own lives.

Cultivating an internal locus of control is an important step to feeling more in charge of your own life. Clearly, you have to be realistic. Thinking that you are going to become a world class tennis champion or guitarist is not realistic for most people. Neither will a positive attitude protect you from all of life's negative events. However, with some practice you can take more **control** of things that are important to you.

Exercise

Practising One New Behaviour

1. Think of something that you would like to change in your life. It need not be something work related. It could be something to do with getting more leisure time or fun out of life. It should be something that you feel difficult to get to grips with because the task feels overwhelming.
2. Think of some small action you can take this week which will be a change in behaviour for you and could make your overall task more achievable. Don't pick an action such as joining a gym. It needs to be something which actually involves you performing a new behaviour which you can repeat. For example, let's say that because you have been so busy you have lost touch with a lot of old friends. The task of catching up with them all feels overwhelming because there are so many people and so much news to catch up with. Set yourself a goal of phoning one old friend this week and having an unhurried conversation with them. I would recommend planning to do your action early in the week as there may be a reason you can't achieve it, e.g. in my example they could be out when you phone.
3. If you successfully performed the behaviour then repeat it the following week and then the week after that and so on.
4. Re-evaluate yourself in the light of having performed your behaviour regularly. In my case if I get back in contact with my friendship network I can re-assess my view of myself that I am not capable of maintaining my friendship networks while leading my busy life as an academic. Think about how **your** ability to **achieve a small change** in your behaviour and **maintain that change**. Think about how the change affects your overall view of yourself, what you are capable of and who you are.

Exercise

Do an 'I Did' List

Credit for this idea belongs to blogger James Altucher (2014) though I have adapted his idea into an exercise for social workers. Altucher stated that 'to-do' lists are dispiriting. We will always have more on our list than we can actually achieve in a day. As a result we will end the day feeling disappointment as we have not achieved what we set out to do. Instead, Altucher suggests that we should write out at the end of the day a list of things that we actually achieved. He states that this list will always be bigger than we expected it to be because most people don't realise just how much they do in a day. Many of the things we achieve will be things which were not on our to-do list because they are responses to contingencies or emergencies.

Your response to this suggestion is probably to say that you need your to-do list because it helps you to set priorities and helps you to remember to do important things. I will be suggesting alternatives to a to-do list in a later chapter. If in the meantime you feel you need to keep your to-do list then do so but try to do an 'I Did' list as well.

Create a table in Word like the one below.

Table 1

What I did	What was the action in response to	What the action achieved	How it contributed to larger or longer-term goals or how I feel about having achieved it

1. End your working day 15 minutes early each day and take the time to fill out this table. In the first column write the actions you performed. Obviously you are not going to want to write absolutely every single phone call or email so pick up to 10 actions which you feel were particularly important or significant. They might be big tasks like writing a report or smaller tasks that were significant such as having a conversation with a colleague that you had been nervous about. Some could simply be things which took up a lot of time. In the second column write down what the action was a response to. Here, you can indicate whether it was an action which you planned or something which was done in response to something unexpected. In the third column write down what your action achieved immediately. In the final column write down how your action may have contributed to a longer-term or over-arching goal. For example, it might have improved your working relationship with a service user or put something in place which will prevent a problem developing in the future.

2. Spend a few minutes thinking about what you have achieved today and how you feel about your achievements.

(Continued)

(Continued)

3.   Repeat this process every day for at least a fortnight. You may or may not want to continue doing this beyond two weeks but hopefully doing it regularly for a couple of weeks will have helped you to see just how much you do.

4.   At the end of two weeks reflect on how you have been using your time and think about which things that you have done are the most effective uses of your time. Also consider what your lists tell you about how much you are in control of your work. If lots of your entries in column 2 are unplanned then think about whether any of these unplanned events or interruptions could be pre-empted; for example, diarying in a regular meeting with someone rather than waiting for them to call you at a time which might turn out to be inconvenient. This is where your final column comes in to play as you can give yourself credit for achieving actions that reduce the need for work further down the line.

Chapter recap

In this chapter we have introduced the concept of emotional labour as an inherent source of stress in social work. This form of stress is inevitable because of the nature of the social work task and the types of problems which we work with. We have also looked at some of the stresses caused by socio-economic factors and changing social policy; although not inherent to the social work process these compound the stressful nature of the job. I explained the physical and psychological effects of stress and listed some symptoms of stress to look out for. I then asked you to do an exercise which would assess the degree to which you feel able to be in control of the direction of your life and gave a couple of exercises which can help you to build a sense of your own volition.

I hope you have learned from this chapter that by making small changes to your behaviour you can change how you begin to feel more in control of your life and grow in confidence about changing other behaviours.

Next up!

In the next chapter we are going to look at the concept of resilience and why it is important for social workers. We will look at vulnerability to stress, question whether some people are luckier than others and consider how we can build our own personal resilience. All the main psychological elements that make up resilience will be introduced and I will suggest some exercises which will help you to build up these different components of resilience.

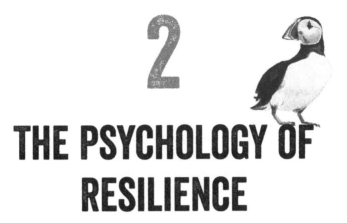

2

THE PSYCHOLOGY OF RESILIENCE

Key Concepts and Issues in this Chapter

- What is resilience and what does it mean for you personally?
- Individual and environmental factors in vulnerability and resilience
- Model for understanding vulnerability to stress
- Fine tuning our understanding of resilience
- Building self-confidence
- Building self-esteem
- Building self-efficacy
- Building tolerance of frustration
- Building a resilient attributional style
- Building optimism
- Building hardiness
- Building an ability to interpret stressors as challenges rather than threats
- Building an active coping style
- Building a willingness to accept, admit and show vulnerability
- Building a resilient social support network
- Building and maintaining focus in our life
- Building personal intelligence
- Building spiritual resilience

What is resilience?

In Japan in 2011 (CNN, 2011) a huge tsunami was set to hit the island of Oshima. The fishing community who lived there were all in danger of losing their fishing boats through having them dashed against the harbour or the land. Most people on the island headed for the hills to avoid the terrible devastation which would accompany the giant wave. One man, Susumu Sugawara, a 64-year-old fisherman ran to his boat and set sail for deep water. Susuma considered that he must sail directly into the wave. He believed that this was the only way to save his boat and preserve an all-important link with the mainland for his community. I don't know enough about the physics of tsunamis to know if this was just an act of defiance or a logical strategy but what I can say is that it must have taken incredible courage.

We can only imagine what it must have been like to face a 20-metre wall of water. Sugawara said in the CNN interview that he talked to his boat. He said, 'You've been with me for 42 years – if we live or die – we will be together.' He then pushed on 'full throttle'. After the first wave there was a giant drop down and then four more giant waves. Throughout it all he maintained his steely determination – and came through unharmed.

By successfully riding the tsunami, and enduring wave after wave, he saved his boat. After calm returned he was able to use his boat to transport people and supplies between the island and mainland. He became a local hero, working tirelessly with his boat to maintain that vital link that his community needed.

Sugawara-san didn't run away from his problem or try to pretend it didn't exist. He faced it down and won through. He had a resilient state of mind.

In this chapter we will look at what resilience actually means and what constitutes a resilient mind.

Exercise

Resilience

1. Think of as many words and phrases as you can which describe for you elements of resilience
2. Try to come up with a single sentence which defines resilience for you.
3. Come up with as many reasons as you can for why resilience is important for social workers.

Keep your answers to these questions for future reference as we explore the concept of resilience in this chapter.

Vulnerable groups or vulnerable individuals?

An important question to ask first in considering what is resilience is whether resilience (and conversely vulnerability) are properties of individuals or groups of people or both.

The relationship between adverse social circumstances and psychological distress is well understood by psychologists and social workers. For example, Lewis and Sloggett (1998) found that one in seven men who become unemployed will develop depression within six months. They also found that job insecurity was a risk factor for depression. Most social workers will be familiar with the study into social adversity and depression by Brown and Harris (1978). They found that depression in women was associated with significant adverse life events in the previous year, such as being responsible for the care of young children, the absence of a supportive intimate relationship and the early loss of their mother.

More recently, Lindert et al. (2014) carried out a meta-analysis based on 19 studies involving over 115,000 participants. They found evidence of a relationship between experience of sexual or physical abuse in childhood and anxiety and depression in adulthood.

None of these results will be surprising to social workers as an understanding of the structural and social causes of physical and emotional ill health is fundamental to social work training. What is less well covered in social work training are individual differences in how people respond to stressors. Data about social groups can help us to understand why a particular social class or group of people are more likely to suffer from poor mental health. What it does not tell us is why some people who belong to disadvantaged groups fail to develop psychological problems while some people with an advantageous economic or social position nevertheless develop psychological problems. To understand this we need to look at individual factors which affect psychological vulnerability.

Model for looking at the relationship between individual and environmental factors

In thinking about the complex relationship between individual factors and mental distress it can be helpful to use psychological models. One such approach is the 'vulnerability-stress model' of the development of psychosis (Fowler et al., 1995). Within this type of model individuals can have an underlying genetic or biological predisposition to suffering mental illness, and a degree of risk associated with personal psychological factors. As environmental stressors increase then people with progressively lower levels of predisposing factors can fall victim to a serious mental illness. We can look at this as a useful model for explaining the relationship between individual factors and social stressors across a wider range of psychological problems. We all have some degree of vulnerability to stress, and a degree of protection through close relationships and social networks. However, as stress levels increase then more and more people face the possibility of suffering from a psychological problem.

People's habitual responses to threats and opportunities will affect their ability to deal with these situations effectively. Are our habitual responses helpful or unhelpful to us?

The illusionist Derren Brown (2011) in an episode of his Channel 4 series visited a town to demonstrate his views about the existence of luck. His proposition was that there was no such thing as luck but rather that it was some people's optimism and positive responses to opportunities which made them appear to be lucky. He used an example of a town resident who was extremely cynical and considered himself unlucky. Brown presented the 'unlucky' person with a number of opportunities, all of which he failed to take advantage of. He even went as far as placing a £50 note in his path, which the 'unlucky' person did not even notice. This was contrasted with another 'lucky' individual who made the most of an opportunity which was offered to them. Rather than success being a matter of luck in this experiment, it was a matter of whether the individual was able to recognise opportunities and had the necessary self-confidence and optimism to take advantage of them.

A similar issue applies to how we view other people's motives towards us. If we are chronically suspicious of other people we will miss out on opportunities to build friendships and personal and professional relationships.

None of the above should be seen as implying that we should be unrealistically optimistic or naively trusting. Rather I am saying that a positive, open approach to life is likely to lead to greater resiliency than a closed and pessimistic one.

In this chapter we will consider how we regularly deal with the world and consider whether there might be ways that we can change how we habitually think about and respond to stresses and frustrations in our life.

Exercise

Responding to Stressors, Opportunities and Challenges

Here are several ambiguous scenarios. For each one I would like you to write down what your initial thoughts would be. What would your initial internal dialogue be? You might find it useful to do this with another person and compare your answers for similarities and differences.

1. An opportunity arises in your department for a secondment to a job which involves a greater amount of responsibility than your current job and a temporary increase in salary. It is in an area which you are very interested in and would significantly raise your profile as you would report directly to senior management. Note: if you already hold such a post then imagine an opportunity to do a job with a national profile.

2. Your manager sends you an email saying that s/he wants to speak to you urgently.
3. As you walk down a street you see several of your friends having lunch together in the window of a cafe but you had not received any prior invitation.
4. You are asked to re-write a report which you have spent a great deal of time drafting.
5. You have planned a day to get some admin cleared, but one hour after arriving at work you receive a call about an emergency which you will have to deal with.

For each scenario think about what your initial thoughts might be. How else might you think about each situation? What strategy would you use ultimately to deal with each of the situations? What differences were there in your responses and anyone else's whom you did the exercise with? How helpful do you think your responses to these situations are in terms of responding positively to opportunities, handling crises and maintaining your self-esteem? Are any of your responses to these scenarios indicative of how you respond to situations you find yourself in within your own life? Do you think your style of responding is consistent with a resilient state of mind?

Please keep in mind your answers to these questions as we consider the meaning of resilience.

Defining resilience

Earlier in the chapter I asked you to come up with a definition of resilience. Now, here are a few definitions of resilience from the literature.

The first is a definition by Michael Neenan and Windy Dryden from Neenan (2009: 17).

Resilience comprises a set of flexible cognitive, behavioural and emotional responses to acute or chronic adversities which can be unusual or commonplace... While many factors affect the development of resilience, the most important is the attitude you adopt to deal with adversity. Therefore attitude (meaning) is at the heart of resilience.

You will see that as cognitive therapists Neenan and Dryden put a strong emphasis on how we interpret events. From this perspective, resilience involves reflection on our experiences and an ability to understand them or reinterpret them in ways which are psychologically beneficial.

The next definition is by Kate Murray, Alex Zautra and John Stuart Hall in Zautra et al. (2010: 4). Their definition draws in turn on the work of Masten (2001), Rutter (1987) and Bonanno (2004).

In our view resilience is best defined as an outcome of successful adaptation to adversity... Two fundamental questions need to be asked when inquiring about resilience. First is recovery, or how well people bounce back and recover from challenge. People who are resilient display a greater capacity to quickly regain equilibrium physiologically, psychologically and in social relations following stressful events. Second, and equally important is sustainability, or the capacity to continue forward in the face of adversity... We ask how well people sustain health and psychological well-being in a dynamic and challenging environment.

This definition conceptualises resilience as a homeostatic process – our ability to keep ourselves on an even keel or at least return to stability quickly. Murray et al. also make reference to the concept of 'reserve capacity', that is that we need to have additional psychological and physical resources to deal with unexpected or unusually severe demands. This is an important concept to bear in mind when thinking about the most demanding jobs in social work such as child protection. If we are working at the full extent of our capability all of the time, then where can our reserve capacity come from?

Further insight into the meaning of resilience comes from Southwick et al. (2011: xi–xii) who expressed the view that resilience is 'multi-dimensional and dynamic'. By multi-dimensional they mean that people can show resilience in some elements of their life but show greater vulnerability in others. For example, they may be better able to cope with stress and trauma in their work life than their home life or vice versa. By dynamic, they mean that people may show greater resilience at some stages in their life than others or different degrees of resilience in the face of different types of problems.

People will vary in terms of the support which they receive from their family, their friends and their community. Are the shared beliefs and attitudes of their community or their immediate social circle helpful in building and maintaining their resilience?

Racism, sexism and other forms of discrimination can all erode people's capacity for resilience. Our religious and cultural environment can either help give us a positive self-identity, or be a source of oppression if our lifestyle choices go against cultural norms. These refinements add nuance and complexity to our understanding of resilience and go beyond the intrapsychic definition of Neenan.

We can and should try to re-interpret our experiences but getting help from other people is important too.

Reflecting on the meaning of resilience

At this point I would like you to go back to the definition of resilience and the elements of resilience you listed in response to the exercise at the beginning of this chapter. How much did your answers agree or differ from the definitions given above?

Now return to the exercise on responding to stressors, challenges and opportunities. Do you feel that your style of responding to the scenarios is indicative of good resilience? Do you have 'reserve capacity' to deal with unexpected or

unwelcome situations? Do you have the positivity of mind to deal calmly and constructively with challenges and seize opportunities or is this something you need to
develop further? In the next part of this chapter we will look at ways of building
a more resilient mind.

Building resilience

In this section we will look at how you can build a more resilient state of mind based
on what we have found to be key components of resilient thinking. You can choose
which of the areas of resilience are most important for you. It is not going to be
possible to work on all these areas at once.

Richardson (2002: 313) stated that 'there is a force within everyone that drives
them to seek self-actualisation, altruism, wisdom, harmony with a spiritual source
of strength'. From this positive, humanistic approach we will look in turn at various
aspects of building a resilient mind.

Building self-confidence

Self-confidence is an important resource for tackling the demands that are made of
us in our professional role.

If we can project self-confidence then this will instil confidence in service users
that we know what we are doing and that we are capable of acting in their best interests. This in turn will make it more likely that they will confide in us, co-operate with
the help we are giving them and take our advice seriously. It will also make it more
likely that other professionals will trust us. As a result they are more likely to take
our concerns seriously and provide help and support from their service when needed.
An ability to project self-confidence is therefore important to our productivity and
our ability to gather resources for our service users and co-operation from other
professionals. It is important to note that projecting self-confidence does not involve
bluffing or arrogance. Rather, self-confidence allows us to admit to the things which
we do not know without feeling ashamed.

Approaching a new task with confidence

Here is a staged approach to tackling a new role or task in our work with confidence.

1. Having realistic expectations of ourselves

A lack of confidence is often allied to fears about making a fool of ourselves or
falling short of our expectations of ourselves. Often perfectionist thinking and

unrealistic expectations are a source of low self-confidence. We often judge ourselves much more harshly than we would judge someone else in a similar situation. We can diminish some of these fears by setting out realistic expectations for ourselves. If we are doing a task for the first time then realistically we are not going to be as polished at it than if it was a task which we have a lot of experience with.

2.   Advance preparation

Nobody ever performs well at something new without a lot of preparation. There are things we can do in advance of the task to help reduce the stress on us when we are actually performing it. We might need a list of prompts to make sure we don't forget an important stage or element of the task. We might need someone else to work with us on the task or at least be available to consult if we get stuck. We could ask someone who is experienced in the task to give us some pointers or advice. Getting clarification of what our role is, how it relates to other people's roles, and what others' expectations are going to be of us is also important. This will help to stop us getting out of our depth or agreeing to things which are not our responsibility. It is also useful if you are working with other people to check whether everyone is in agreement about objectives and find out if anyone has any personal or professional agendas which might not be immediately apparent to us.

3.   Creating a positive vision of ourselves doing the task

One useful technique when preparing for a task which we have anxieties about is to find a quiet place to sit and relax. We should then try to visualise ourselves performing the task confidently and successfully. While we are doing this we should try to breathe slowly and calmly and relax our whole body. The idea is to get ourselves accustomed to the idea that we can accomplish the task successfully and imagine what that would look like. If it helps, and you don't feel too self-conscious, then you can rehearse out loud some of the things that you might have to say such as introducing yourself to other people or describing your role. Practise saying these things until your speech flows naturally and confidently and get used to hearing yourself speak in a way which projects confidence.

4.   Arrive on time and calm for your task

If you are feeling anxious about doing something then allow extra time between the difficult task and the one before it and make sure that you know where you are going and how to get there.

5.   What to do if things go wrong

The most important thing to do if you make a mistake is not to catastrophise. Even the most experienced professional will make an error from time to time.

The important thing to do is to recognise that you have made an error, apologise for it and take corrective action. My favourite musician is an American singer–songwriter Todd Rundgren. Todd has a very long and diverse repertoire, built up over 45 years, which he enjoys dipping into randomly. As a result he sometimes makes mistakes or forgets bits of lyrics. His way of dealing with errors is to apologise, make a joke at his own expense and then start the song again. His use of humour gets the audience on his side and his underlying confidence in himself as a musician enables him to quickly recover and resume his performance. A single mistake (or even several on a new task) is not a sign of incompetence provided we are open about it and take corrective action. Most of the time our colleagues want to see us succeeding and will help us when we make a mistake, forget something or need assistance. If you approach your work with humility, eagerness to learn and warmth towards others then there will always be someone to help you when you need it.

Exercise

Building Self-confidence

Imagine you are going to chair an important meeting such as a case conference. There will be lots of people there who you do not know and whose job roles you may be unclear about. You will have to ensure that the meeting sticks to task and that there is a clear conclusion with everyone being sure of their responsibilities. You also have to ensure that everyone, especially service users or lay people, gets a chance to have their views heard.

If you are experienced in chairing case conferences in multi-disciplinary environments then consider how you might chair a meeting which is outside your comfort zone such as an inquiry or a meeting which takes evidence from national experts.

- What expectations would you have of yourself in performing this task?
- What preparation would you undertake in advance of the meeting?
- What sort of image would you like to conjure in your mind of yourself completing the task?
- How would ensure that you got to the meeting on time and unflustered?
- What sort of things might go wrong at the meeting and how might you deal with them in a way which is not defensive or aggressive?

Now reflect on the answers which you gave. Are they reflective of how you normally deal with new situations? For example, do you always prepare adequately?

If you found this exercise helpful then try it with a real-life example of something which you are going to have to tackle shortly in your own job or course.

Building self-esteem

Carl Rogers was a famous humanistic psychologist and therapist who was both influenced by and was influential on social work.

Rogers (1959) said that people can be given what he called conditions of worth during their development. That is, they are led to believe that they are only a worthwhile person if they behave according to certain expectations and requirements of those who are bringing them up. For example, a parent might want their child to be ambitious or feminine or have the right kind of friends. When the child deviates from these requirements then affection might be withdrawn. This leads to the child feeling that they are only a good person when they behave according to other people's expectations. This can be become a habitual tendency and can rob people of their self-esteem or prevent them from feeling they are free to make their own decisions. An important part of Rogers' therapy was to give people acceptance within the therapeutic relationship. He referred to this acceptance as unconditional positive regard. That is, the therapist will value the person as an individual without putting any conditions on them. This freedom from judgement gives the client a safe space to explore what their needs are.

Not all of us can afford therapy nor necessarily want to go into it. However, we can reflect on our sense of self-esteem and consider why it may be less strong than we would like. Many of us spend large amounts of time feeling guilty about our imperfections and dwelling on all the instances in which we fall short of our ideals. Logic tells us that this is self-defeating. There are very likely to be things which we could do to improve our health or other aspects of ourselves. However, this is only going to be worthwhile if we actually think that we are worthy of loving care in the first place. Any road to improvement must therefore start from a position of loving the person we are at the moment.

We need to accept the person that we are as worthwhile before we can move forward in a positive way. We need to let go of our conditions of worth. We need to let go of negative self-judgements. This is not easy. As Molden and Hutchinson (2008: 60–1) observed 'The nature of any belief is that once formed it attracts evidence to support it and deletes anything to the contrary. It may be a tenuous belief but we like to defend our beliefs and will go to great lengths to do so'.

Developing a more positive self-image is something which we have to work at consciously and it requires thought and reflection.

Building self-efficacy

I introduced the concept of locus of control in the first chapter. I said that people with an internal locus of control believe that *people generally* can influence what happens to them. Self-efficacy is a related concept but its not the same thing. Self-efficacy is the belief that *you personally* have the *ability* to *achieve* positive changes in your life. One normally has to have an internal locus of control to have a strong sense of self-efficacy. However, it is possible to have an internal locus of control *and* poor self-efficacy. The latter would be the case if you believed that you should be responsible for what happened to you yet felt ill-equipped to achieve positive outcomes for yourself. An internal locus of control coupled with low self-efficacy is likely to lead to poor self-esteem. It is also the case that an external locus of control coupled with a low self-efficacy could accompany high self-esteem as the person would just blame others for what happened to them. The best combination is therefore internal locus of control, a high (but realistic) sense of self-efficacy and a positive (but not fragile) self-esteem.

Benight and Cieslak (2011) stated that positive self-efficacy is positively correlated with job performance and job satisfaction. If we have a strong belief in our ability to achieve results then this will make us more motivated to initiate and follow through positive actions in our work which will in turn lead to better performance and greater satisfaction. Benight and Bandura (2004) proposed that *coping self-efficacy* was related to our beliefs about our abilities to cope with trauma or stressful events.

Exercise

Building Self-efficacy

Imagine you have been shortlisted for a new job, which is a very exciting opportunity for you. At the job interview you will be asked to explain how you had overcome challenges in your existing job. Think about and write down three challenging situations you have had to deal with in your existing job. Try to make the three challenges as different as possible. Now, list all the skills you deployed in overcoming each of the challenges. What new skills did you achieve or demonstrate for the first time in overcoming each challenge? What does your ability to rise successfully to these challenges tell you about yourself as a worker and a capable person? Are you a stronger and more competent person through having overcome these difficulties? Write a short reflective piece which covers these points.

Hopefully, having done this exercise will help you to realise how you are growing and becoming more capable through dealing with challenges. You will also have some good examples of dealing with challenges which you can use in job applications or interviews.

Self-efficacy is not about accomplishing the impossible but rather having a belief that you have the psychological and physical resources to respond to challenging situations.

Building high frustration tolerance

Neenan (2009: 74) defined high frustration tolerance (HFT) as 'the ability to endure in times of stress or upheaval without continually complaining how difficult the struggle is and lapsing into self-pity every time a new setback is encountered'. Neenan considers tolerance of frustration to be an important strength underpinning resilience.

Over the years I have often heard colleagues saying that it is 'great to have a good moan'. They are wrong. While it is positive to identify problems and then take responsibility for tackling them, constant negativity in the absence of action saps people's motivation.

Ricard (2009) described a process which a friend who is a development worker in Nepal goes through when he arrives at a new village. He stated that initially he is assailed by people giving him reports of their own problems. He quickly shifts the discussion by asking people to describe what their talents, abilities and resources are. He then asks them to imagine what they can achieve with these assets and moves rapidly on to getting a commitment from them to achieve these objectives. From this he launches a programme of work within a matter of days. Such fast-paced change is likely to be slowed by the bureaucratic organisations that employ most social workers. However, tapping in to people's positivity is still going to be more fruitful than indulging a culture of negativity.

Another technique to deal with feelings of frustration is to visualise your frustration as a dark cloud that will drift across the sky and be replaced with sunshine when it goes away. If you are doing something like driving which requires concentration then always pull over into a safe place before doing any kind of visualisation technique.

Building a resilient attributional style

David Burns (2008), building on the work of Aaron Beck, described how people who suffer from depression regularly make cognitive errors in how they interpret events which happen to them. These thinking errors are self-defeating and are implicated in the maintenance if not the origin of depressive states of mind. All of us can make thinking errors of this nature even if we are not actually clinically depressed. It is worthwhile developing an ability to recognise and neutralise these self-defeating patterns of thinking as they represent an obstacle to the maintenance of positive self-esteem and our ability to brush off minor rejections and disappointments. I would recommend getting a copy of Burns' book *Feeling Good: The new mood therapy*, especially if you are working in the mental health field. It is very accessible and can be useful to lend to service users who are 'cognitively minded'.

Here is my commentary on some of the common cognitive errors, adapted from the work of Burns and Beck:

1. Over-generalisation

This involves developing a general rule based on one occurrence of an event or one piece of evidence, e.g. 'I was rejected for this job because of my inexperience – therefore I will be rejected for every job I go for on the same basis.'

2. Filtering

This means paying attention to negative aspects of our performance or feedback we have received while ignoring the positive elements. For example, our tutor or manager may have given us a mixture of praise and criticism about an essay or report that we have written. Filtering involves becoming despondent about the elements of our performance which were criticised while ignoring or forgetting the elements which we received praise for.

3. All or nothing thinking

This means having a very dichotomous view about something with no shades of grey. For example, we may feel that if we are not perfect at our job then by definition we are useless. We could apply this thinking to our role as a parent or any other role we have in our life. It leaves very little room for failure. If the only alternative to being perfect is to be useless then inevitably we will come to categorise ourselves as failures.

4. Personalising

This is accepting responsibility for something which is not our fault. For example, sometimes unassertive managers are afraid to tackle people who perform badly directly and instead send out critical emails to a whole section or department.

Someone who is prone to personalisation will automatically assume that the critical comments are directed at them. Somebody who personalises will tend to assume that when anything goes wrong then it their fault.

5. Catastrophising

This means jumping to the conclusion that a minor mishap will surely lead to disaster.

6. Emotional reasoning

This involves mistaking feelings for evidence of facts. For example, we might believe that because we feel we are useless at something this means that we are in fact useless. There are times when our feelings are a useful source of information. For example, we would conclude that a comedian was good because they made us laugh. Similarly, being anxious about a yawning precipice in front of us is useful because it makes us cautious about walking near to it. However, when anxiety and fear get the better of us they can reinforce incorrect views about ourselves.

7. Mind reading

This involves making assumptions about other people without any evidence. For example, we might think that our partner is displeased with us because they are not very talkative when in fact they themselves may be preoccupied with something which happened at work. The problem with mind reading errors is that if we speak or behave in accordance with false assumptions which arise from them then we can compound the misunderstanding by reacting defensively or aggressively.

8. Fortune telling error

This involves assuming that we are unable to change or improve an element of our performance in an area in which we feel that we lack competence and that we will always be bad at it.

9. Using 'should' statements

These are statements which place unrealistic expectations on our own or other people's behaviour. Examples are 'I should be slimmer'; 'My partner should be more intuitive about my needs', etc. When we apply these statements to ourselves they cause dissatisfaction with who we are and can lead to poor self-esteem. When we apply them to other people they can lead to resentment, miscommunication and conflict. 'Should' statements are based on arbitrary sets of rules which we have set in our mind about how we and other people ought to behave. When they come into conflict with reality they become a source of disappointment or resentment. We should challenge these statements when we apply them to ourselves and question their reasonableness when we apply them to other people.

10. Magnification/minimisation

Magnification is where we exaggerate the importance of a mistake we make in a social encounter such as accidentally spilling a drink. Minimisation would involve disregarding or de-emphasising the positive feedback which we receive from other people when they give us praise.

There are similarities and cross-over between these different types of cognitive error. There are also a few others which I haven't chosen to list because of space or because they would take us into an abstract discussion which would detract from the main points I am trying to make.

The importance of learning to recognise these cognitive errors is that they help us to spot where our thought processes are working against our psychological wellbeing.

Once we have gained an understanding of cognitive errors we can try to operationalise these insights using a technique that Neenan (2009) refers to as ABC thinking. A = the activating event or adversity which we encounter; B = the beliefs or attitudes about what happened at event A; C = the emotional or behavioural consequences of our beliefs about the event. Neenan states that we frequently respond to events by missing out the B stage. We assume that the event itself has led to how we feel or how we responded. However, our response to an incident is going to depend on what meaning it has for us. If we are making cognitive errors in how we process things which happen to us then our reactions to them are going to be disproportionate or inappropriate. We may be unduly critical of ourselves, or fail to realise just how much others hold us in esteem.

Having a positive view of ourselves is important to the development of resilience and using an ABC approach can help us to see how negative emotions and anxiety are frequently the result of faulty interpretations. We can use the B stage to try to think clearly about why a particular event made us feel unhappy about ourselves. We can then challenge our conclusions and try to develop more positive ways of viewing ourselves. Learning to challenge negative thinking patterns is an important way of building our self-esteem and self-concept and in turn building resilience.

Exercise

Building a Resilient Attributional Style

Think about an incident which has happened to you recently and which left you with negative feelings about yourself. It could be a remark which somebody made to you or perhaps how you performed in a task at work. Try to think about what conclusions you drew about yourself as a result of the incident. Did you make any of the thinking errors identified by Beck? Are your negative feelings about yourself a result of what actually happened or are they a result of how you interpreted the events? What other ways could you have interpreted the event? Can you choose an interpretation which acknowledges areas where you can grow but which is consistent with a positive self-image?

If you are struggling to find an interpretation of your event which is more generous to you then try imagining that the same incident had happened to a friend of yours. Would they have felt as badly about themselves as you have? How might they have interpreted the incident?

If you can develop a regular practice of examining negative feelings about yourself and reinterpreting them in a more positive way then this will help you to develop your resilience in the face of psychological setbacks.

Building optimism

Feder et al. (2011: 17) defined optimism as 'the inclination to adopt the most hopeful interpretation of any event' and stated that it was associated with greater life satisfaction in addition to greater resilience.

The difference between optimism and pessimism is sometimes defined as whether one believes that a glass of water is half empty or half full. I would argue that the optimist is the person who has the faith that s/he can refill the glass from a tap or failing that has the drive to go in search for a well. Optimism should not be thought of as a passive, static or intrinsic quality. It is something which can and should be cultivated and should be translated into action where there is a possibility of change.

Mathieu Ricard (2009), a Buddhist monk, described how he was met with a tirade of pessimism when he described his plans to build a school in Tibet. He was told that he would be refused official permits, be fleeced by contractors and fall victim to local corruption. Four years later he had built, with the help of benefactors, sixteen health centres, eight schools and twelve bridges. His way of dealing with officialdom was often to ask for permits after facilities had been built. Through diplomacy and demonstrating to local authorities that he was achieving objectives which made them look good, he managed to get officials on his side. For Ricard, *resolve* is a crucial component of optimism because it is needed to convert positive thinking into action.

Ricard also identified *adaptability, serenity* and *meaning* as components of optimism in addition to *resolve*.

He defined *adaptability* as an ability to be constructive and creative in the face of obstacles rather than resorting to avoidance or escapism.

Serenity is the ability to remain calm and composed in the face of threats which we can't do anything about and face our failures with quiet acceptance when we have done all that we can.

Meaning is 'realising the potential of every human being, regardless of his or her condition'. This is a humanistic value as well as a Buddhist value. It was my own personal faith in the capacity of individuals for change that led to me becoming a social worker.

Taken together, Ricard's components turn optimism from a state of mind to a form of action.

Building hardiness

Miller and Harrington (2011) described Kobasa's (1979) concept of hardiness as a combination of personality characteristics which act as a resource for people when they are facing stressful life events. These characteristics are *commitment, control* and *challenge.*

Commitment is about having a purpose to one's existence which we have a determination to fulfil. Social work should contribute towards us having positive purpose in our life. If we do not feel that this is happening then we should consider whether there is a problem with the particular post that we are in or our attitude towards it.

Control was defined by Miller and Harrington (2011: 63) as one's 'perceived ability to influence one's destiny and manage experience'. This is a similar concept to locus of control.

Challenge is one's ability to see change as an opportunity for growth and renewal rather than as a threat. We are currently seeing a lot of change in social work in terms of new ways of funding and managing the profession such as social work practices, payment by results, etc. A willingness to look for new opportunities in this rapidly changing environment is likely to be a more resilient response than seeing all these changes as completely negative, regardless of our views about the politics behind the changes.

Hardy individuals will see change as inevitable and seek to engage with it constructively. Miller and Harrington stated that a number of studies have found hardiness to be a factor which limits the effects of stress on physical and mental health. It is something we should cultivate.

Building an ability to interpret stressors as challenges rather than threats

In the previous section we found that one component of hardiness was an ability to see stressors as a challenge. Similar ideas have been developed by others.

Benight and Cieslak (2011) discussed Lazarus and Folkman's (1984) transactional theory of stress. Within this model stressful situations can be appraised as challenges rather than threats if the individual believes that there can be a positive outcome from overcoming them. The idea of conceptualising obstacles as challenges was central to Ryan Holiday's (2014) book *The Obstacle Is the Way*. Building on the Greek philosophy of stoicism, Holiday advocated that we thrive in life because of what we overcome rather than thriving in spite of what we overcome. He quoted the Emperor Marcus Aurelius who said, 'The impediment to action advances action. What stands in the way becomes the way.' We all express this sentiment when we speak in job interviews about how we have overcome difficult situations in our work. Situations which seemed at the time to be an obstacle to us eventually become part of our marketable skills once we have overcome them.

Our ability to conceptualise stressors in this positive way is dependent on our attributions about the cause of the stress and our ability to tackle it and the amount of reserve capacity we have to tackle it. It is much easier to view a unique or short-term stressor such as a difficult case or a difficult meeting as a challenge than it is a chronic stressor such as a high caseload. If we can successfully accomplish a difficult piece of work then we will feel that we have achieved something worthwhile and added to our experience. Keeping up with unfair or unrealistic demands on a constant basis is unlikely to lead to the same feelings of achievement. Not all obstacles can easily become part of our 'way' but for certain types of stressor it can be a useful way to think about them.

Building an active coping style

The Japanese fisherman who was mentioned at the beginning of this chapter was someone who literally approached his problem head on. You hopefully won't have to face a problem of the magnitude of a tsunami but there is a lot to be gained from an active engaged coping style. Feder et al. (2010) identified planning and problem solving as important components of resilience. Rather than trying to ignore, deny or suppress worries and problems we should try to proactively face up to them.

Gerard Egan, in his book *The Skilled Helper* (2013), outlined a simple yet highly effective problem-solving model. His model is useful for therapists and social workers who are working with people who want to achieve change but you can use the same approach to thinking about how to achieve change in your own life. The technique involves thinking about a problem in three stages. In the first stage the problem is fully defined, clarified and explored. In the second stage we actively explore how we would like things to be in a more satisfactory situation. In the final stage we develop strategies for getting to our goal.

The central point in Egan's model is that people frequently jump from being unhappy with something to making a decision or a change. However, we may make the wrong decision or take the wrong action if we have not properly thought through what we are trying to achieve by making changes. We could end up going from one unsatisfactory situation to another. By properly exploring the problem and thinking through how we would like things to be different we can ensure that we make changes which bring us nearer to an alternative goal.

Other forms of active coping include using *humour* to help take the fear out of worrying situations and improving our *physical fitness* to help us better cope with what life throws at us.

Feder et al. (2011: 17) describe humour as 'one of the most mature defence mechanisms' and an important tool in warding off depression. They also point to optimism as an important factor in resilience and greater life satisfaction. They refer to evidence from neurobiology that humour and optimism are associated with increased activity in areas of the brain associated with processing positive emotions. Thus, positive thinking can have biological effects on the brain.

Building a willingness to accept, admit and show vulnerability

If you spend time with cats you will have observed them rolling over and displaying their tummy. When a cat has been fighting and feels defeated or outclassed it will use the rolling over behaviour to show submission. By showing its tummy and leaving its vital organs unprotected it is showing that it is no longer a threat. This will normally result in the other cat backing off because it feels it has won and its dominance has been acknowledged. Cats use the same manoeuvre with people to show that they trust them. If a cat shows this behaviour it is an invitation for you to pet them – but not necessarily on the tummy, so watch your fingers.

Sometimes an important aspect of resilience in humans is being able to admit that we are feeling overwhelmed and we need help. Like cats, we need to have ways of signalling our vulnerability to others so that we can get help.

Other parts of this chapter have emphasised the value of showing confidence but this is not a good strategy if we are genuinely out of our depth or sinking. Being able to ask for help is not something all of us find easy to do. Acknowledging to ourselves that we are not coping is a difficult barrier for many people to overcome.

Good friends and colleagues and/or a strong partnership are all valuable sources of feedback about how we are coping. If people whom we trust are telling us that we appear stressed, edgy or out of character then we should listen to them. Also invaluable is a trusting relationship with our supervisor, manager or tutor. If we have a relationship of trust with our colleagues and our manager in which we can talk about how we are truly feeling then this is a very important resource. However, it requires being honest with ourselves and being able to communicate openly with others that we need their help. Being able to show vulnerability is not a weakness whether you are a man or woman. Rather it is a way of showing others that we trust and value them.

Building a resilient social support network

As social workers we are very aware of the importance of social networks in supporting people who are experiencing stress or adversity. Feder et al. (2011) summarised a number of studies which demonstrated the importance of good social networks and secure attachments in protecting against stress-related disorders.

Skodol (2010) said that 'pro-social personality traits' such as *sociability, emotional expressiveness* and *interpersonal* awareness all contribute to emotional resilience.

People high in *sociability* are extroverted, friendly and gregarious.

Emotional expressiveness refers to the ability convey one's emotions appropriately.

Interpersonal awareness is an ability to be genuinely interested in others, be empathic towards them and convey this warmth and understanding to them effectively. People who lack social skills can receive help with them and there are many self-help books and sources of information on the internet which can help.

One of the problems with work-related stress is that it can actually lead to us neglecting our social networks at the very time we need support from others most. If we are feeling worn down by work we may feel that we don't have the energy to go out and spend time with people socially. If we are suffering from depression we might lose the ability to enjoy leisure activities. We might even start to believe that we have nothing to offer other people because we are depressed and over-involved in work-related problems. We may snap at our partner if they tell us that we need to relax. Thoughts or behaviours of this nature are signs that we are suffering from stress. We need to slow down and take steps to re-establish our equilibrium.

An important part of maintaining our capacity for resilience is actively maintaining our social life and social networks. If we are temporarily too busy and don't have time for meeting friends or having a phone call then it might be a matter of posting on Facebook, texting or messaging a friend. The important thing is to maintain our emotional connections with people in some manner and let them know they still have you as a friend if they need you.

Building and maintaining focus in our life

Maintaining a focus or purpose in our life is also important for resilience. This idea was introduced in the earlier section on hardiness. A purpose or focus can help protect people after a traumatic event. For example, some people who have lost a relative to an accident or a disease get involved in campaigning to raise money or awareness for others who face a similar plight or work towards changing the law.

For some people a faith or a belief system can help to anchor them. Religions can involve rituals or practices which can help to build positive states of mind which contribute to resilience. For example, Buddhist meditations involve developing feelings of loving kindness to the self and others and overcoming negative emotions.

Pargament and Cummings (2010), in reviewing the literature, found evidence that by providing a belief in the meaningfulness of life religion may help to preserve people's psychological wellbeing and be a buffer against stressors. Religion also gives a number of people a sense of identity, a connection with their community and access to a social network. For many social workers their faith will be an important part of what motivates them to work in the helping professions. For others a commitment to a secular belief system or a political orientation may be important to their identity as social workers. Maintaining a psychological connection to the beliefs and values which are important to us is an important way of maintaining resilience.

Building personal intelligence

Personal intelligence is a different concept from either intelligence as we think of it conventionally or emotional intelligence. As described by Mayer and Faber (2010) it consists of a heightened awareness and understanding of our own personality and an ability to utilise that awareness to problem solve and live more congruently. I think personality intelligence might be a more appropriate term.

The model of Personal Intelligence described by Mayer and Faber (2010) consists of four 'areas'.

Area 1: Identifying personal information

This is an ability to gain accurate insight into our own personality by introspection and accurately interpreting feedback from other people. Are we, for example, able to judge when someone is teasing us about an aspect of our personality versus try-ing to politely point out a failing? Conversely, do we disregard real compliments which are given to us as throwaway remarks? Does our own estimation of our abilities accurately reflect how we are seen by other people? – 'To see oursels as ithers see us' (Burns, 1786).

The better we are at being able to accurately identify our true personality characteristics, the better we will be at utilising them in times of adversity. This area also involves being able to identify personality-relevant information in situations of stress or adversity. This will help us to identify threats and opportunities.

Area 2: Developing models of the self and others

This involves using characters or archetypes to help us to understand elements of ourselves. By internalising these characters or objects with which we identify, they become a medium for gaining a better understanding of ourselves and also in expressing our beliefs, attitudes and traits. We can have identifications with fictional characters, real people and product brands which reflect aspects of who we are. The changing nature of these identifications can help us to understand the development and changes in our personality as a result of experience. Block and Turula (1963) stated that internalising the strengths of people we admire can improve our resilience. This process of internalising the values and characteristics of others can be compared to the development of the super-ego (morality) in Freud's developmental theory, though it covers all aspects of personality rather than just morality. Furthermore, this perspective suggests that personality development is a lifetime process rather than one which ends on attaining adulthood. As we incorporate values, attitudes and behaviours of others whom we admire we can become more psychologically secure and draw wisdom, strength and strategy from them.

Thinking about my own internalised characters, many of them are characters from comic books and TV shows which I grew up with and some are real people who I admire. The superheroes who I grew up with taught me a lot about how to deal with adversity, overcome personal disadvantage, and stand up for justice for others who are persecuted or victimised. From 1970s television I was influenced by the character of Kwai Chang Cain (from the series *Kung Fu*), who used mental calm and non-violence as powerful tools in achieving positive outcomes for others. From the science fiction series *Space 1999* I was given a model of leadership by the character Commander Koenig who would have a very inclusive style to his decision making.

From real life I try to emulate the calm reassuring self-confidence of President Barack Obama in my public speaking balanced with some of the quickfire wit of comedian Jerry Seinfeld.

Another part of my identity is my love of world music, which is an expression of my desire to reach out for new experiences. It is also an interest which I have developed with my wife so it is part of our identity as a couple.

Faber and Mayer (2009) described five key archetypes which people identify with: the magician (wise, sage-like characters such as Gandalf, Professor X and Mr Spock); the striver (heroes including superheroes and mythological characters); the carer (lovers and caregivers); the conflictor (outlaws and anti-heroes, e.g. Walter White in *Breaking Bad* or Vic Mackey in *The Shield*), and the everyperson (representations of the average man or woman). Our choice of archetypes not only reveals things about our own personality but also about how we view the world and the way people relate to each other.

Area 3: Using archetypes

The characters which we identify with can become internalised guides who can help us to make positive decisions in times of adversity. We can think about what a particular character or archetype might do in a given situation.

Area 4: Being able to make sense of our life story and understanding what has been significant for us in terms of life events and our psychological life

This involves reflecting where we have come from; considering which elements of our life have been influenced by different archetypes which we have taken into ourselves; how our beliefs and attitudes have grown and changed through experience; and where we are headed.

The whole essence of personal intelligence is about making us more resilient through understanding who we are and what strengths and ideas we have internalised.

Exercise

Building Personal Intelligence

1. Spend 10 minutes creating a list of fictional characters and real people who you think represent bits of yourself. Don't think about this too hard. Use hot cognition. The characters and figures who come to mind easily are going to be the most important ones. Don't try to come up with a list that will impress other people. I was honest with you about my nerdy tastes. Allow yourself the same amount of honesty.
2. Try to make a list of what good qualities and abilities of these characters and people you are able to deploy in your work and in other areas of your life.
3. Write down how you think that you assimilation of different characters and people might have affected you developing personality and how you have responded to different obstacles and opportunities in your life.
4. Come up with a plan of how you can positively take your life forward over the next five years with the help of the different positive qualities which you have assimilated.

Building spiritual resilience

Mindfulness is a concept from Buddhism which has been incorporated into cognitive behavioural therapy (CBT) over the past decade or so. The rediscovery of ancient wisdom and its adoption by a very scientifically driven form of therapy is quite remarkable even if it isn't appreciated by everyone. I remember being in the book room of a CBT conference and overhearing some participants whispering their irritation about books about Buddhism sitting beside very scientific books. The success of mindfulness in this extremely rational field is testament to the value of the ancient wisdom of Buddhist psychology.

Moffitt (2009: 65) stated that an important part of mindfulness is *Sampajanna* which he defined as 'the ability to see clearly what needs to be done, what you are capable of doing and how it relates to the larger truth of life'. It involves acknowledging how our emotions have arisen and understanding the thought processes which underlie the emotions. This process of understanding the relationship between thoughts and feelings is similar to the CBT process of identifying cognitive errors which we discussed in an earlier section.

One way of developing mindfulness is the process of *cultivating stillness* as described by Carroll (2009). He said that we are frequently faced in our work (and this applies especially in social work) with difficult practical and ethical decisions. We may find ourselves paralysed about making a decision in case we either take too great a risk or take too safe an option. Alternatively, we make a decision in haste without properly evaluating whether our thinking is clear. Cultivating stillness is all about taking a moment to clear the fog from our mind. It involves putting aside the emotions which are crowding our mind and allowing us to have space and clarity. To practise stillness, what we have to do is to switch off all our inner chatter and mental noise and just experience what is around us in that moment. What can we see? What colours? What textures? What sounds can we hear? Can we hear our own breathing? Can we see something that we haven't noticed before? By allowing ourselves to live in the moment we can then move towards acknowledging what anxieties, fears and emotions are affecting how we are thinking and behaving. We can take ourselves to a calm space from which we can make a wise decision.

When I teach resilience I ask students to go somewhere quiet on the campus for 15 minutes and just try to take in all that is available to their senses. Only a few students successfully complete the exercise – given that we are located in a busy city not all the sights and sounds they experience are pleasant. However, they do get the chance to experience a different state of consciousness in which they can appreciate the world in a different way.

Most people, however, don't do the exercise and I find them talking with friends or smoking. Stillness is not something we find easy in our fast paced, over-stimulated existence. How easy do you find it to commit a short time to experiencing stillness? Can you see the value in it?

If you want to explore mindfulness further you could consider trying to learn some Buddhist meditation practice. This usually involves cultivating an ability to concentrate the mind on one thing – usually our breathing – and widening this out to other levels of awareness. A full description of this is outwith the scope of this book but there are classes available in most communities and there are books which describe meditation practice too.

I hope you have enjoyed exploring different elements of the psychology of resilience. In the next chapter we will move from psychological resilience to looking at how we can maintain our physical resilience.

Chapter recap

In this chapter I asked you to think deeply about the concept of resilience and consider what it means for you personally. We then considered how the way we view the world not only affects how we feel about our life but what we actually experience. I then introduced a range of components which make up the psychology of resilience. I gave some suggested exercises to help you to develop some of these components. If you read through the chapter in one sitting then you probably did not have enough time to do all the exercises. I would recommend coming back to the chapter several times and doing these exercises in stages.

Further reading

This chapter relies significantly on ideas from cognitive behavioural therapy. If you want to learn more about the relationship between thoughts and feelings then I would recommend *Feeling Good: The new mood therapy* by David Burns. It is a classic work and is useful equally to therapists, social workers and lay people. It explains cognitive theory in an easy accessible manner and is full of insights and useful advice.

If you would like to read more about Gerard Egan's problem-solving model then his book *The Skilled Helper* gives a comprehensive explanation of his model and how to use it.

If you would like to learn more about mindfulness or meditation then many Buddhist organisations run introductory meditation classes which you can attend for a suggested donation or reasonable fee. There are also people independently running classes in mindfulness or meditation. Some are reasonably priced though I have seen quite exorbitant fees being charged by some. There is no reason to pay excessively large fees for this type of course so look around at what is available.

You may also want to investigate the phone app Headspace which offers guided meditations and help on mindfulness.

Next up!

In the next chapter I will look at work/life balance and how to achieve it in the era of electronic communication. How do we experience inner peace when we are at work and surrounded by stressors and the demands of others? What is vicarious trauma and how does it affect social workers psychologically? We will also look at the importance of physical health and how we can ensure that we get some exercise and enough sleep.

The chapter kicks off by asking you to think about what your aims in life are from a personal and professional point of view and how to deal with situations where our professional values and aspirations are not being fulfilled at work.

3

VALUING OUR OWN HEALTH AND WELLBEING AND IMPROVING WORK/LIFE BALANCE

Key Concepts and Issues in this Chapter

- Determining priorities for our work and personal lives
- Inner expansion as a technique for expression of the self
- Cultivating inner stillness
- Creating boundaries between work and personal life
- Developing your inner sanctuary
- Developing the right sort of passion about social work
- Coping with vicarious trauma
- Getting enough sleep
- Getting enough exercise
- Positive intelligence and gratitude

What is it all for?

Many of you will be familiar with the TV drama *Breaking Bad*.

In the course of the drama Walter goes from being a mild-mannered school teacher with cancer to becoming a ruthless drug baron. At different times he tries to convince other people and himself that he is doing what he is doing for the best interests of his family. In the final episode, however, he admits that he was really working as a criminal because it made him feel good rather than for any more unselfish purpose. Even his final confession that he did it for selfish reasons could be seen as partly a delusion for he is acting to feed his ego rather than the totality of who he is and who he has been. As the series progresses, the warm considerate part of him disappears as he is consumed by demons which are driving him. Feelings of inferiority about his status, resentment of the success of his former business partners and anger about his illness are all part of what drives him forward. In this sea of anger and delusion he loses sight of the real love and respect which the important people in his life have for him. He is someone who has lost all focus and perspective on his life and its purpose.

Arguably, one of the reasons that mindfulness has come to prominence in recent times is that it helps us to understand what we are doing with our life and why we are doing it. Are we really being true to what we want to achieve for ourselves, our family and the people we work for or are we thrashing around in a sea of delusion? The character of Walter White had many good things in his life – his family and his work as a teacher, and the offer of financial help from a former associate. However, he could not see the value of any of these things.

Exercise

Understanding Your Priorities for Work and Your Personal Life

Find some quiet space for yourself.

- What are the three things in your work life just now which you value most?
- What are the three things in your life outside work which you value most?
- What are your three biggest goals for your work life over the next five years?
- What are the three biggest goals for your life outside work for the next five years?

In answering these questions try to be as broad in your answers as possible. For example, getting a job which is home based could be a goal whereas getting a specific job with a specific employer which was home based would be too narrow a goal.

Having written your three lists think about where goals might be in conflict or might support each other. For example, if you enjoy face-to-face work with service users then a

(Continued)

(Continued)

goal to achieve promotion may result in a loss of that interaction which you enjoy. On the other hand, if you enjoy mentoring newer staff then that might support a goal for promotion to management. Alternatively, if you enjoy both these things then it might suggest that you should consider a job role which involved some management/mentoring while maintaining a small caseload. Think also about where there may be conflict between work and your personal life either in your present situation or in terms of your goals for the future. What can you do to get these conflicting priorities back into balance? What sort of compromises might be necessary to achieve work/life balance?

Only you can make the decisions about what is most important to you in life. Different readers will reach different conclusions about the relative priorities of work and professional life. However, what is important is that we are aware of where these priorities are and do not become like Walter White obsessively chasing delusional goals.

While Walter White is an extreme case of disconnection between goals and who we are, Leider and Buchholz (1995) described a more common phenomenon called rustout syndrome. They described this as a state in which people are no longer growing, because they made choices which had given them security and financial success but not a sense of achieving things which they find significant. Social work is a career which most of us enter into with a strong sense of purpose. We want to make a difference for others and tackle injustice and discrimination. Sometimes the mundane nature of casework, the lack of resources, and bureaucracy can be crushing. Gergen and Vanourek (2015) suggest an approach which they term 'pervasive service'. This involves finding creative ways in all areas of our lives to make contributions to our communities and the world. If our job is not always giving opportunities to do things which we find inspirational then we can make up for that in other areas, such as running a race for charity or getting involved in the work of a local voluntary sector agency in our spare time. They also suggest that we should try to find an organisation or a team to work with that shares our outlook and priorities. In large organisations, the culture can vary greatly between sections. I have worked in organisations where some teams have genuine camaraderie while other parts are blighted by bullying and unfairness. Getting a role in a team and an organisation which is consistent with our personal values is important for all employees and especially so in a job like social work.

Taking the concept of 'pervasive service' a stage further, the Dalai Lama and Howard Cutler (2003) explored the idea of 'inner expansion' whereby we track the things that are important in our job role back to what they mean for us at a fundamental level in our being. Thus, for some social workers their job might be an expression of their wish to fight oppression. For others it might mean helping to give people back a sense of control of their life. For me personally, social work is about enabling people to make choices and giving them the psychological help or material resources to live their lives according to what is important to them. While all social workers follow a common code of ethics and values, they will differ in which elements of the job are important to their identity at a fundamental level. Following the Dalai Lama's principles we can base our identity on the essence of what our work means to us in the totality of our life rather than on the external form which it takes in our current job role. By gaining this understanding we can then make sense of where our existing job role fits with our own identity and where it might come into conflict. For most people, there will be a degree of compromise between the essence of who they are and the degree to which they can express it in their job.

Exercise

Inner Expansion

Take some time to think about what fundamental values you have as a person. How do these values relate to how you see the world and the behaviour of other people? How do they relate to your views on politics, if politics are important to you? How do your values relate to your spiritual life (if you believe that you have one)? How do these values, ethics and political views form part of your overall identity as a person?

Now think about your current job. To what degree and in what ways is it a vehicle for expressing and practising the things that are of fundamental importance to your identity? To what degree is there conflict between your job role and your personal identity?

Now think about the totality of your life and your other roles: for example, as a spouse, parent, son or daughter, carer, volunteer, member of a community, member of a team or club, political activist, church member, union member, blogger, etc. What opportunities do you have for expressing your identity in areas of your life outside work?

Now thinking about your life as a whole, do you feel that you are able to express who you are fundamentally within your life to an acceptable degree? If not, what changes might you have to make either in your work life or other areas?

Being able to see the connections and disconnections between our life as a whole and our identity is in my opinion very important to professionals in human services. I feel it is especially important to social workers at a time when there is a perception that the values of our profession are at odds with current political trends. Tummers et al. (2013) described a phenomenon called policy alienation in which professionals are in a state of 'psychological disconnection' from the policies which they are being asked to implement within their job. As public policy diverges more and more from the values and traditions of a profession, feelings of despair and alienation for those in the profession can increase. Being able to identify the ways in which we can or cannot express our core values and identity in our life as a whole can help us identify more clearly our sources of satisfaction and our sources of dissatisfaction and disconnection. This in turn can help us to make informed choices about the direction of our life.

Cultivating inner stillness

Being in touch with our values and thinking about how we can apply them in our lives requires a degree of awareness and a capacity for reflection. I introduced the concept of inner stillness in the previous chapter. Here I explain how it fits into the wider aspects of self-awareness.

Lawrence Boldt (1993) described three keys from the Japanese Samurai code of Bushido which are important to channelling energy effectively: being present, being concentrated and being strong. Being present means having an inner stillness which allows us to be conscious and alert. Boldt states that most people 'muddle through life half asleep, scarcely aware of the dangers and opportunities that lie all around them' (p.63). Being still and alert allows us to respond to the world as it really is rather than being influenced by our own misconceptions, anxieties or fears. Concentration is the art of perfecting an ability to do one thing perfectly and carrying this ability to focus into other parts of our life. We can develop an eye for detail or a discipline in one area of our life, be it a sport or an art or a craft and then apply the lessons from that into doing our work more skilfully and mindfully. Strength refers to strength of the body. This means having a body which does what we require it to rather than a body which limits us. Most social workers spend their time with more cerebral activity and are very far removed from physical caring. This is unfortunate because physical caring can be a very intimate and spiritual experience. The lack of physical labour combined with the strong demands of the emotional labour in social work makes for a poor balance of energies. Getting the necessary physical activity to maintain a balance in our life is a difficult but important task.

We have a choice between having a life which is healthy and purposeful or mistreating our bodies and muddling through life aimlessly. To have real purpose we need to develop that stillness and awareness which Boldt referred to. This is difficult when we work in a culture where activities such as smoking, excessive eating and drinking are seen as aids to relaxation. Whatever you gave as your goals for work and the rest of life in the previous exercise I am fairly sure that they will involve you having to maintain good health, unless all you want to do is lie in bed and watch TV. Maintaining health should therefore be a priority for all of us.

Making a clear division of space between work and the rest of life

An important stage in being able to relax is making space for it. A few years ago I saw what I thought was very poor advice in a publication I normally have a great deal of respect for. A reader had asked the *Financial Times* agony aunt whether they had to check their emails on holiday (Kellaway, 2013). The agony aunt declared that the reader ought to check his emails on holiday simply because 'everyone else does' since the advent of the work Blackberry. I was pleased that reader response was more balanced. Some readers suggested that it might be warranted simply because the reader worked for a small business and there may not be suitable cover for their expertise. However, many readers believed that holidays should be sacrosanct. This is very much my view. Many people already have personal worries when they go on holiday, e.g. about the health and wellbeing of relatives left at home. I feel that a holiday should at least be a complete break from work, even if it is not a complete break from all our worries. I would also suggest that before a two-week holiday you clear your diary for the two days immediately preceding your holiday to deal with unexpected contingencies. It is also useful to clear your diary for a couple of days after the holiday to deal with the email backlog and any report requests which have come in while you were away.

Making appropriate space for relaxation outside of vacation times can be more difficult. The availability of electronic devices has made work more flexible for many people. However, it can also lead to work pressures becoming tyrannical and omnipresent. Gergen and Vanourek (2015) suggest that it is important to have a daily routine which timetables in time for exercise, relaxation and reflection. Obviously there will be times in a job such as social work in which emergencies and other contingencies will interfere with our ability to find time for relaxation. However, if we make a regular place for relaxation and exercise in our schedule then there is a better chance that we will achieve it some of the time. Gergen and Vanourek term rest and relaxation 'daily renewal'. Another part of daily renewal is making time to eat properly. This means eating away from your desk and taking time to eat slowly and chew properly.

Having some time away from your office or work routine is also valuable. Making time in the day for a walk in the sunshine or a visit to a small exhibition in a local gallery are examples of renewal. If you work on an industrial estate then bring a book to absorb yourself in for 20 minutes or go for a short walk if there is some green space nearby. Many people do not realise that they only have to walk a short distance from their office to find a country lane. Even if you work in a city then there will be interesting things to see just a short distance from where you work. When I worked in Sunderland I found many interesting sites around me. There was a building called the Eagle Building that had a slightly comical statue of an eagle on its roof. There was also a building with carved elephants on the outside at first floor level. This had been an establishment called The Elephant Tea House in the early part of the nineteenth century. Seeing it evokes images of another era and sights like this lift my spirits when I feel bogged down by the bureaucratic parts of my job. Cities like Manchester are full of gems like these – all it takes is a willingness to look up or look around and take in your surroundings. If you can find enjoyment in what you see then this will be part of your renewal.

Gergen and Vanourek also mention the concept of 'sanctuary' which is about having some sort of activity in which you can really lose yourself. You may not have time for this sanctuary every day. It might be something you can do in small bites over the week or might be something you do in longer chunks at weekends. The important thing is to get absorbed into it and take your mind away from whatever problems may be troubling you at work. For some this might be walking, running or cycling. For others it might be prayer or meditation. For yet others it may be a hobby such as painting, photography or bird watching. The important thing is to get that space and refuge from work. If you can enjoy the feeling of being completely absorbed in an activity which you enjoy then you will be giving your mind and body time to heal from the emotional stresses and strains of working as a social worker.

Exercise

Developing Your Inner Sanctuary

The next time you are doing something that you really enjoy and find fulfilling, take a few moments to take in all the aspects of how you feel within your mind and body. What is your breathing like? Is it calm and regular? Are your muscles relaxed or tense? What can you hear? What can you see? Are you looking at something which fills you with joy or wonder like a beautiful sunset or painting? What is it about this experience which special?

Then, a day or two later try to recapture that feeling when you are somewhere else such as at your desk at work. Try to remember what made the positive moment special. Try to relax your breathing so that it is just as it was when you were doing what you enjoyed. Try to recapture a feeling of wonder if you were looking at something beautiful or inspirational.

Practise reaching back to that relaxed feeling whenever you feel stressed, overworked or undervalued.

Developing the right type of passion about your work

Social work is seen by most social workers as a calling or a vocation. It is something which we feel very passionately about. Kaufman (2015) suggests that passion for work can be a negative trait if it leads to people becoming obsessive and unable to switch off. He calls this obsessive passion and points to research which suggests that it is implicated in burnout. Kaufman suggests that rather than arising from feelings of joy about one's work, obsessive passion arises from people's work forming a large part of their self-concept. Thus, if their ability to focus on work is threatened then this is experienced as an attack on their identity. Kaufman contrasts this with the concept of harmonious passion. This involves an ability to bring one's work life into harmony with the rest of one's life and switch off when it is time to enjoy free time or time with one's family. This can be difficult when we work in a job which involves complex and distressing human problems. However, it is an important skill to develop.

Social workers who see their job role as a central part of their self-identity are in my opinion especially at risk from feeling dispirited by attacks on the profession in the press and in society more widely. I consider that one way to deal with this issue is to embrace Gergen and Vanourek's (2015) concept of pervasive service and take the view that our passion for helping is part of a much wider theme in our life than simply our present job or even the job title of social worker. Thus our values are not dependent on our ability to do our job as it exists now. The increasing fragility of job roles and organisations will be discussed in a future chapter.

Trauma and social work

Van Heugten (2011) discussed the impact on social workers of 'vicarious trauma'. She described this as the 'emotional impact of working with, listening to and observing trauma experienced by others, and absorbing this trauma into one's own psyche via a pathway created by empathy' (p.113). At an extreme level Van Heugten suggests that this can resemble PTSD but that it can be experienced in much less severe ways and that different workers are affected to different degrees. She explains that less experienced workers, less supported workers and those with high caseloads are most likely to be affected severely. She further reports that work by Hesse (2002) and Tham and Meagher (2009) has found that child care social workers are most particularly at risk. This is associated with activities such as removing children from their parents, especially when this is soon after birth, and dealing with sexual abuse. A more recent source of distress for child care social workers is the naming of them on anti-social-work social media sites. Child care social workers also live with the threat of being openly criticised in the media over perceived failings in their practice when harm comes to children in their care.

Van Heugten also reports that for all types of social worker working with terminally ill service users and coping with the suicide of a service user can be particularly traumatic. I have personally experienced the latter and therefore recognise how shocking and upsetting this can be. Despite the fact that social work is a profession concerned with helping people the level of support offered to social workers who experience vicarious trauma can often be completely inadequate. Even with good support it may be necessary to supplement support at work with help from a counsellor. Good employers provide access to an independent counselling service for their employees via the Human Resources department. If this is not available then a private counsellor or therapist can be contracted by the social worker, though this can be expensive.

Van Heugten says it is important for social workers to develop the ability to modulate their responses to trauma so that they can provide empathy while being able to emotionally differentiate themselves from their service users. She suggests that it is important to embed an understanding of vicarious trauma in social work education as well as an ability to identify signs of psychological disorders such as anxiety and depression. She states that workers should have the opportunity for time out following the witnessing or vicarious witnessing of a traumatic event, but at the same time not being isolated from colleagues who could provide emotional support. Opportunities should be available for discussing or reflecting upon the events without being forced into having a detailed debriefing.

In the next two sections we will look at general self care which is important both in recovery from trauma and in maintaining our fitness for the regular demands of social work.

Getting enough sleep

Former British Prime Minister Mrs Thatcher famously managed with only four hours sleep a night. As this is a social work book I probably don't need to say anymore to convince you of the benefits of a good night's sleep. A scientific study (Knapton, 2014) suggests Mrs Thatcher's limited need for sleep could have been the result of having a gene which allows the body to survive on less sleep. For the rest of the population there is divided opinion about how many hours of sleep are needed. Some experts say that everyone needs at least eight hours per day, while others claim that what is more important is the quality of the sleep and that it is undisturbed. Sleep is a time to rest and repair the body and also to process information and experience from the day. Since social work is a job which involves exposure to stressful and emotionally demanding situations the role of sleep in processing the day's events is especially important. Lack of sleep has also been linked to increased likelihood of obesity. There are also studies suggesting that exposure at night to light sources such as computer and phone screens suppresses the production of melatonin which controls sleep and waking cycles (Wallop, 2014). Some people deal with these issues by having a certain amount of time free of electronic screens before going to bed.

Whatever your views about exactly how much sleep is needed it can certainly be agreed that social work is a job which requires alertness and concentration from the point of view of one's personal safety and also to avoid making serious errors in our practice. Of course, social workers cannot always make decisions which lead to positive outcomes. However, if we are rested and capable of concentrating properly then we are less likely to overlook important information, policies and protocols in reaching our decisions.

Getting enough exercise

This is a subject of a great deal of wasted money (gym fees) and broken resolutions. Many people make very bold and unattainable resolutions about improving fitness which inevitably lead to disappointment and disillusionment when they are not attained. A few years ago the UK pharmacy chain Boots introduced a health improvement campaign to the public as part of its health education called 'Change One Thing'. The concept was that it would be easier for people to improve health-related behaviours if people focused on just one thing at a time. Changing entrenched behaviours is very difficult as we have had many occasions on which to practise the unhealthy behaviours. For a new behaviour to become part of our habitual routines takes a great deal of practice. If we are used to slipping out of the office for a cigarette or a cake after a stressful conversation or phone call then we will probably find ourselves repeating this behaviour without even having to think about it. We may therefore have to put quite a lot of concentration into defeating a single bad habit. Cognitive behavioural therapists recognise that the best source of motivation is to have small successes and build upon them. Thus, rather than motivation leading to achievement, a change in behaviour (albeit small) must precede motivation. If we are going to have any success in improving our health and our wellbeing then it is important to give ourselves praise for what changes we make no matter how small and ensure that these changes are permanent.

Friedman (2015) stated that while it is difficult to find time against a background of pressing deadlines and work demands we should consider what we mean when we say we don't have time to exercise. He suggested that what we really mean is that it is not a priority. He considered that we should instead view exercise as an essential part of our job. He outlined the many ways in which exercise can improve job performance:

- Better concentration
- Sharper memory
- Faster learning
- Prolonged mental stamina
- Enhanced creativity
- Lower stress
- Elevated mood

While Friedman was not writing specifically for social workers I think we can agree that these exercise-related enhancements are all ones which are beneficial to the practice of social work. Friedman suggested that an important factor in ensuring that we take up exercise is that we focus on activities that we will find enjoyable. For example, I enjoy circuit training and running but I find exercise machines such as cross trainers and treadmills incredibly boring. I am more likely to persevere with the types of exercise which I enjoy than those that I don't. Being able to get a form of exercise that you can stick to or build upon depends on you finding the exercise enjoyable and having a feeling when you are finished that you have accomplished something worthwhile.

There are a number of phone apps which can help you build up workouts and monitor your progress. S Health for Samsung Galaxy phones, for example, allows you to monitor your steps if you have a walk and it can also help you to monitor your calorie intake. Social media can help you to get support from friends. Some apps can post your progress directly onto Facebook or other social media and hopefully some up-votes from friends will give you some encouragement. Training for a charity event like a charity run can also be a motivation for improving fitness even if improving your condition for the sake of your health isn't.

Positive intelligence and gratitude

We normally think that if we achieve our goals then this will make us feel happy. Achor (2012) argued paradoxically that it is satisfaction with our life that leads to success. This idea is similar to that we discussed in relation to exercise; that we have to change our perspective before we can achieve more. But how can we feel better about ourselves if we are fundamentally dissatisfied with elements of our lives and have a habitual tendency towards negative thinking patterns? Achor suggests that humans have a very high degree of neuroplasticity and that we can train our brains to think differently if we apply ourselves. He suggested that we should engage in a positive behaviour at least once a day. If we repeat this process regularly over a period then it will cause a change in our psychological outlook. He reported that he asked a group of taxation managers with a leading accounting firm to do one of five activities daily for three weeks. The activities they could choose from are as follows:

1. Write down three things you are grateful for.
2. Write a positive message to someone in your social network.
3. Meditate at your desk for 2 minutes.
4. Exercise for 10 minutes.
5. Take 2 minutes to describe in a journal the most meaningful experience of the past 24 hours.

Achor compared the activities group with a control group in scores for optimism and life satisfaction immediately after the programme finished and then again at four months after the programme finished. At both times the experimental group scored significantly better in these important measures of happiness. Achor stated that life satisfaction is a strong predictor of both happiness at work and productivity. The fact that the increase in positivity continued well after the programme had finished suggested that the people in the experimental group had experienced a permanent change in how they thought about the world. Just as negative thinking patterns can become entrenched, so with practice we can develop habits of positive thinking. These positive thinking habits can help us to enjoy and appreciate our lives and achieve more in our work.

The daily positive activities listed above do not cost any money and only take a short amount of time. Why not try one or more of them out daily for a three-week period?

Replacing complaining with gratitude

One of Achor's positive exercises listed in the previous section is that of writing down things we are grateful for. Workplaces can be full of negativity. Our negative self-talk affects our own wellbeing. When people's resentments and frustrations are voiced regularly to colleagues without being challenged then they can form a psychological pollution in the workplace. This can lead to an environment in which negative talk becomes the norm. While there can be a certain amount of solidarity and camaraderie around shared misery, the overall effects of this sort of communication are detrimental. We can change our own internal dialogue by replacing negative self-talk with thoughts and feelings of thanks for things that make us happy or make our lives special. We don't need to actually thank someone in person. It might be that one of the things that makes our life enjoyable is the work of a musician or writer or artist who is no longer alive. We can't thank them in person for their work. However, we can give thanks in our mind for the pleasure which their work has given us. Alternatively, we could phone a friend who we haven't spoken to for some time and tell them why they are important to us or remind them of a time you spent together which has a special memory for you. When we get in touch with happier or gentler times, we can melt away the tension, anger and frustration which has built up in us. Business writers James and Claudia Altucher (2014) recommend carrying out what they call a 'no complaints diet'. They suggest trying to live a whole week without making a complaint about anything. They recommend suppressing any negative thoughts which arise and avoiding conversations in which we might feel social pressure to be negative. They also suggest replacing negative thoughts which arise with feelings of gratitude or compassion for others. If you break the diet and make a complaint then you have to start again at day 1. At the end of the week the Altuchers suggest that you should take stock of how it felt to go a whole week without making any complaints. If it was helpful to your emotional wellbeing, then try to cultivate a non-complaining approach as a longer-term strategy.

The importance of gratitude and positive feelings towards others is an important part of many religions. Buddhism, for example, has a specific meditation, the *metta bhavana*, which is concerned with developing unconditional loving kindness towards others. The Dalai Lama (Gyatso, 1999: 132) said of compassion '...when we reach beyond the confines of narrow self-interest our hearts become filled with strength. Peace and joy become our constant companions. It breaks down barriers of every kind and in the end destroys the notion of my interest as separate from others' interest'.

Compassion and gratitude may sound like soft emotions but they have an important role in the development of resilience.

Chapter recap

The chapter started with a challenge to you to think at a fundamental level about what your life is actually about and what is really important to you personally and professionally. The opportunity to think about our goals in life is theoretically always with us but the pace of life is such that we can find ourselves carried away with events and out of touch with what is important to us. We discussed ways of maintaining our connection with personal and professional values in the context of a policy climate which is antagonistic towards it. We then went on to look at how to maintain physical and psychological health while doing a job which brings us into the contact with the distress and trauma of others. The chapter ended with a reflection on the benefits of feeling gratitude for good things which we have in our life.

Further reading

The book *Social Work Under Pressure: How to overcome stress, fatigue and burn-out in the workplace* (van Heugten, 2011) looks at the different sources of stress which social workers face and some practical ways of tackling it.

I would recommend tuning into James Altucher's daily podcast Ask Altucher available from The Stansberry Radio website. This podcast has helpful advice to workers in any field about how to get their life in balance while being effective and imaginative in how they approach their work.

The Art of Happiness at Work by the Dalai Lama and H. Cutler looks at the spiritual dimension of work and is going to be of interest to anyone who is concerned with being in touch with the ethics and values of their job while trying to find contentment and fulfilment in what they do.

Next up!

In the next section we are going to look at lots of practical suggestions for how you can become more efficient, more effective and have the time and energy for large and important pieces of work. It's all about planning and having the right scheduling tools to make it all possible. We will also look at how to leverage short periods of 'found time' which would otherwise be unproductive. We will also look at why people procrastinate and how we can tackle difficult and complex tasks proactively. The concept of Lean management will be introduced and you will be challenged to look in detail at how some of the procedures could be used in your day-to-day work and how they could be made more efficient.

TIME MANAGEMENT

Key Concepts and Issues in this Chapter

- Reviewing your time management skills – diagnostic inventory
- Dealing with unfeasible workloads
- Avoiding over-committing
- Prioritising your work
- Defining and scheduling actions for 'to-do' lists to achieve progress
- Bringing realism to your schedule
- Exploring why you procrastinate and developing new, more productive work habits
- Making sure you have energy for important tasks
- Managing meetings to make them short and effective
- Managing your expectations of yourself
- Making use of found time
- Introducing Lean approaches to work and using the Five Whys to eliminate wasted effort

---

We have spent time in the earlier chapters looking at the emotional labour of social work. Emotional labour is by no means the only source of pressure on social workers. The unpredictable nature of the job is also a source of stress. Individual workers can face intense pressure if several of the cases they are working on develop into crisis situations at the same time.

Another current concern is about the high caseloads which many social workers have, which are due to a number of reasons including increased referrals and government austerity measures. There is little that individual social workers can do about central government funding on their own. However, they can have an influence on how they use their own time and try to use their time more effectively. It is of course always important to use time effectively, but this is even more the case when work pressures are high.

Thus, being a resilient social worker does not just involve an ability to deal with the emotional demands of the job. It must also involve an ability to manage one's time successfully to meet deadlines and have contingency time available for the unforeseen crises which will inevitably arise in social work.

I am sometimes shocked when I read about the amount of time social workers are reputed to spend on admin tasks according to articles in social work media. I feel that much of this is due to a lack of provision of appropriate IT resources coupled with a reluctance to engage with technology by some members of the profession. I will discuss this issue in the next chapter. In this chapter I am going to focus on time management skills which don't require the use of any particular technology.

Improving one's management of time is a challenge of similar proportions to losing weight or improving one's fitness or nutrition. It involves the changing of habits and behavioural styles which are extremely well entrenched and in which we may have considerable emotional investment. We may even think that some of our poor habits in relation to time management are an essential part of who we are, rather than just a pattern of behaviour. Vincent Van Gogh is reputed to have said, 'If you hear a voice within you saying that you cannot paint, then by all means paint and that voice will be silenced'. As with other types of behavioural change, which we have discussed in this book so far, the key to changing our beliefs about ourselves is to perform behaviours which contradict these negative or self-limiting beliefs. If we can make even just a small change in how we manage our time then it will help us to believe that other changes are possible. Before we can bring about any change in our time management, however, we must first develop an understanding of why our management time is presently sub-optimal.

Reviewing your time management position

This is an interactive quiz to find out what aspects of your work might be causing your problems in meeting the demands of your work. Each question links to an issue which will be discussed in a later section of this chapter. You can jump ahead to the section which deals with your concerns but I think you will find it useful to read the whole chapter at least once.

Question 1

A) Is your workload reasonable?

Yes   No

B) Do you spend time doing work which should be done by others?

Yes   No

If you answered No to Part A or Yes to Part B then go to Section 1.

Question 2

Do you have problems coping with contingencies such as emergencies from service users or last-minute requests for reports?

Yes   No

If you answered Yes to this question then go to Section 2.

Question 3

Do you have problems with managing your time as a result of not keeping an eye on deadlines or being aware of all the imminent demands on your time?

Yes   No

If you answered Yes then go to Section 3.

Question 4

Do you have long 'to-do' lists which include items with no deadline or review date or which have vague statements about issues which you feel you ought to review at some unspecified time in the future?

Yes   No

If you answered Yes then please go to Section 4.

Question 5

A) Do you frequently struggle with deadlines because you have under-estimated how much time it will take to perform a task or elements of a task or because you have over-estimated how much time is available to do them?

Yes   No

(Continued)

(Continued)

B) Do you run into deadline problems with reports or tasks because of other professionals not doing their contribution on time or quickly enough?

   Yes   No

If you answered Yes to questions 5A or 5B then please go to Section 5.

Question 6

A) Do you find it difficult to get started with certain tasks or find yourself avoiding certain jobs because you are worried about your ability to achieve them or because they are in some way unappealing?

   Yes   No

B) Do you find yourself prioritising routine or easy tasks and then finding you have run out of time or energy for difficult tasks?

   Yes   No

If you answered Yes to Parts A or B then please go to Section 6.

Question 7

A) Do you spend lots of time in meetings which are long or overrun or which have agendas which have little of concern to you?

   Yes   No

B) Do you spend a lot time writing up minutes of meetings, or do you find that meeting minutes prepared by others arrive too late for you to make use of?

   Yes   No

If you answered Yes to Parts A or B of this question then please go to Section 7.

Question 8

Do you frequently have feelings of disappointment over how much progress you have made in a day or over a week?

   Yes   No

If you answered Yes to this question then please go to Section 8.

Question 9

Are you able to effectively make use of 'found time' such as gaps between meetings, cancelled meetings or appointments, time spent on public transport, etc?

   Yes   No

If you answered No to this question please go to Section 9.

Question 10

Do you consciously think about how every aspect of how you do your job could be made more efficient and streamlined?

    Yes   No

If you answered No to this question please go to Section 10.

Section 1: Feasible and unfeasible jobs

Question 1 asks whether your job is actually feasible or not. This is an honest question which is worth asking. I think most of us tend to work on the assumption that if we are asked to do something then it must be feasible. While this might normally be a reasonable starting point there are increasing numbers of public sector jobs in which one person is responsible for an area which might previously have been the responsibility of several other people. I have heard, for example, of social services training sections being reduced from a team of ten to a team of eight to a team of six and so on until there are only two people or even one person running them. Admittedly this sort of change is usually accompanied by outsourcing but that in turn requires additional effort to manage and quality assure the contracts with those who are providing the services. Any of us who have worked in the public sector over the past 10 years will have had the experience of personal job insecurity or working beside those whose jobs are being cut or regraded downwards. Even where there are agreements or controls in place to limit workloads, management will sometimes find ways to circumvent them by loading people with additional tasks which are outside the workloading agreement.

If you answered question 1A with a sincere and considered answer of No, then better time management will not solve your problems.

If your work is unfeasible because of a temporary surge in additional work or additional responsibilities then it is reasonable to ask for some additional support to cover this. An example of this sort of situation is where a sudden change in the law or policy means that a large number of people have to be assessed or reassessed over a short-term period. Another example would be the uncovering of sexual abuse on your patch involving children from multiple families. In situations such as this it would be reasonable for management to take on agency workers to cover the additional workload. If this is not feasible then managers should advise staff as to how they should manage their other work and take personal responsibility for measures such as delaying allocation of non-priority cases. They should not allocate cases which they know that their social workers lack the capacity to deal with.

If reasonable strategies cannot be agreed on to deal with a chronic workload problem it may be necessary for workers to ask for support from their trade union or consider looking for another job.

If you answered Yes to question 1B then the first step to dealing with your problems could be to have a discussion with a manager about the scope of your work. Your manager can then help you with delegating the tasks to others. If you are taking on the work of others because you are unassertive or bad at delegating then this is also something which you should discuss with your manager. You may also want to get support from self-help literature on assertiveness. There are a lot of resources available on the internet, including video material which offers practical help with dealing with difficult conversations at work.

Section 2: Over-committing

Question 2 asked whether you had problems finding time for contingencies and unexpected emergencies. If you answered Yes it may be that you are over-committing yourself. Social work is a job in which unexpected or unplanned events are likely to occur on a regular basis. Years ago when I was a practising social worker, my team manager would review my work every month using a workloading system in which time was allocated to tasks such as writing reports, doing intensive pieces of work, doing assessments, etc. The times allocated to these tasks were reasonable but every month half my time was taken up with tasks which could not have been predicted in my workloading meeting. My workloading should have been based on half my available time. A full diary is not a workable starting point for planning the workload of an average social worker. There needs to be scope for slippage and contingencies.

A common problem with being over-committed is that if we are used to having to rush around all the time we may find it less easy to keep track of what all our commitments are. We may not be aware of just how over-worked we are or we may lose track of what it actually means to have a reasonable workload. This may result in a paradoxical situation in which we are less likely to refuse to take on new work. If you find yourself in this situation it would be useful to take some time out of your diary – say a couple of days – to take stock of what all your commitments are, clear out your email inbox and start prioritising your immediate work commitments and scheduling time to do important pieces of work. If, in doing this work stocktake, you find elements of your workload which are unreasonable or unachievable then start making a list of what these things are. Do some preliminary thinking about what elements of your workload can best be done by you based on your skills and experience and those which fit better with the skillset of colleagues. You can then bring these thoughts to the table in a discussion with your manager. Don't make suggestions on the basis of getting rid of work you simply don't like and don't try to hold on to work just because you enjoy it. If you are genuinely struggling then most good managers will want to try to help you. You will lose their sympathy if it looks like you are trying to get rid of unpopular tasks or unreasonably resisting attempts to have work taken from you because you have a strong attachment to it.

Once you are sure that your workload is reasonable you can now start to plan your use of time in a way which takes account of the fact that significant amounts of your time are likely to be taken up with work which you have not planned for. This means planning your working week in a way which allows you to deal with the unexpected.

If you are planning a day of visits to service users then you should plan in some gaps in the late morning and mid or late afternoon. This will allow you to deal with any visits which take longer than expected. It will also allow you to do an urgent visit to a new referral or do an additional visit to an existing service user who needs an urgent appointment. Another important way of building in contingency time is to try to complete reports well in advance of a deadline. If you diary in time to do an important report the day before the report is due then you will have a serious problem if a crisis arises that day. You may have to end up writing the report at home. If you are regularly finding that you have to do tasks like report writing in your own time to meet deadlines then this is an indication that you are not building contingency time into your schedule.

Section 3: Prioritising

If you answered Yes to question 3 then you may have a problem with prioritising work.

It is likely that our work commitments involve tasks which are of immediate priority, some which have to be completed in the medium term and some issues which we have to deal with in the longer term.

Problems can arise when we let a medium-term priority, such as a report or a review which is due in two months, drop off our radar. Suddenly we find out that the deadline has arrived or passed and it is too late to start gathering the information together to get the report ready in a reasonable timeframe. Problems can also arise when we forget completely about longer-term objectives or issues which require periodic checks or maintenance. For example, we may have noticed a few months ago that the tread on our tyres is starting to get near to the legal minimum or that we need better virus protection on our computer. We may have made a mental note that these are things which are going to require attention at some point in the future but without a system for reminding ourselves we may forget about them. They might only come to our attention again when a Police Officer is writing us a ticket for having illegal tyres or our computer gets infected with a virus and we lose all our data.

We therefore need ways of keeping in control of all these conflicting demands which exist within different priority timeframes. Time management guru David Allen (2001) uses an aerospace analogy based on altitude from the ground to differentiate between different types of priorities. Runway tasks are those which have to be done almost immediately such as urgent emails; 15000 metres in the air is concerned with our very long-term plans for our work and family life. In between there are levels at altitudes of 3000, 6000, 9000 and 12000 metres with the lower levels being short- to medium-term tasks and the higher levels being the medium to long term. The point of the analogy is to help us to see the links and continuities between our immediate priorities and our medium- and long-term goals. They are not separate streams but are part of an integrated whole. If we are attending to the correct priorities in our daily work then we should be contributing to our longer-term life goals but this will only work if we can keep in mind that bigger picture which can only really be appreciated from a high altitude perspective. There is a section below where you can complete your own priorities at each level. My suggestions for issues at different levels are more short term overall than David Allen's would be but that reflects the nature of social work as opposed to the business audience which he is writing for.

Exercise

Viewing Your Workload at Different Altitudes

Try to imagine that you can move towards or away from the ground like Google Earth or that you have acquired the power of flight. Imagine your work life as if it were a landscape with highways, train lines, mountains, trees, towns and cities. When you are near the ground the fine details and small objects which you can see represent your immediate priorities and day-to-day tasks. As you move away you can make out the bigger geographical features which dictate where all the buildings and roads are positioned. Think about how you can plan your medium-term priorities in such a way that they are compatible with the traffic flow of short-term demands. As you get higher think about how the different elements of your work fit together and how they fit into your agency's priorities, your career priorities and, at a still higher level, how they fit with your priorities for your personal future.

Ground level – e.g. read today's emails, complete an urgent report.

Your priorities at ground level:

3000 metres – e.g. scheduling visits to new service users who have been allocated to you, investigating what resources are available for service users who you have recently assessed.

Your priorities at 3000 metres:

6000 metres – e.g. planning a major piece of work with a young person leaving care, planning a complex care plan for a service user with a risk of self-harm.

Your priorities at 6000 metres:

9000 metres – e.g. thinking about how you will settle into and develop a new role or responsibility which you have agreed to take on within your team, beginning a course which will equip you with new skills and thinking about how you will find time for the assignments.

Your priorities at 9000 metres:

12000 metres – medium-term work plans – e.g. planning to become a practice educator or apply for Team Manager's post if you are at that stage in your career.

Your priorities at 12000 metres:

15000 metres – long-term plans for your family life and long-term career – e.g. start a family, become Director of Social Services.

Your priorities at 15000 metres:

Now think about how you can plan your priorities at all the different levels so that your plans make sense from every perspective. If you find this too daunting then just try focusing on the short to medium term for now.

Allen believes that it is important to have a proper method of managing and keeping track of our workload. If we have this then we will not be troubled by thoughts of things which we have to attend to. He stated that we will only be preoccupied with work issues in three situations:

1. If we haven't clarified exactly what outcome we want to achieve or how we are going to achieve it.
2. If we haven't defined the next action necessary to achieve the goal.
3. If we haven't put reminders of what we have to do and what has to be achieved into a system which we trust.

We will consider points 2 and 3 in the next section. For now, the important message is that if we have an effective process for managing our work priorities we can stop worrying about things which we have vague anxieties about and focus on working productively and mindfully in the present.

Section 4: To-do lists and task scheduling

If you answered Yes to question 4 then your to-do lists probably looked a bit like mine did a number of years ago. They went on for pages. Some were items which were due very soon, some were due a significant amount of time in the future and some were just very vague ambitions such as getting my office tidied.

Two important steps are needed to make our to-do list manageable and achievable. In the last section I mentioned that David Allen said that it was important to define the next action that needs to be done to achieve the objective which we are seeking. Allen refers to this as the 'power of next action'. He also states that we need to put in some form of reminder into a 'system'. He is identifying the fact that while we may have many tasks in our head or in a to-do list we may fail to achieve them because we have not scheduled the task in some way and worked out what the immediate action is to take the task forward.

To identify the value of Allen's advice let's use the example I mentioned above of wanting get our office tidied. We might have a vague feeling that our work environment is less pleasant and less productive because it is untidy. We resolve that we will do some work on this when we get some spare time. However, we never seem to find that time and as time goes by the project drifts and our office gets even more cluttered. Alternatively, we may actually find ourselves with a spare hour when we could do some tidying. However, we realise that we have no rubbish bags to put all the junk in and that some of the rubbish needs to go into special bags for confidential shredding. We have to give up on the idea of tidying at this time but make a vague resolve that we will tidy up some other time at which we point we will again find we don't have the rights bags.

The 'next action' approach involves identifying the next step that has to be taken and putting *that* in the to-do list rather than the overall objective. So, the 'next action' for tidying our office would be to order some bin bags and confidential shredding bags. We then need to schedule when we are going to do our office tidy (or at least the first stage in our office tidy if it is a big job). We should pick a time when we know we are likely to have a couple of hours spare. We then have to block that time out on our diary or calendar. If it does not take place for some reason then we need to reschedule it and put in another block of time right away. If we want to track our progress in tidying our office we can put a reminder into our calendar or diary for some date in the future when we will read a message from ourselves which says 'office tidy to be complete by this date' or 'office tidy due in 2 weeks'. Provided we can keep track of these reminders we will be able to see what tasks are due soon and diary in any additional time necessary to complete the tasks. Outlook is particularly good for this as it allows us to put tasks and reminders electronically into our calendar and even record what percentage complete a task is at any given time.

We can use this approach to deal with any task. For quick tasks, which require a simple action which can be accomplished in under five minutes, the simplest method is to do them as soon as we become aware of them. For tasks which require one or two actions but which cannot be done immediately then we can add them to an immediate to-do list and put a reminder on our diary or calendar to do them at a suitable time. For more complex tasks we may want to set up a system of reminders and targets using a diary or electronic calendar and regularly review the progress of the task/project.

Exercise

Changing Your To Do List from a Wishlist to Action Points

If you have a to-do list that has some vaguely defined objectives in it, try creating a box like the one below and defining a 'next action' for each item.

Table 2

Vague Item from To-Do List	Next Action
Example: Become familiar with local services which provide day activities for adults with learning difficulties	Example: Ask a colleague for contact details of any good services for adults with learning disabilities and phone at least one of them to arrange a visit
Your item 1	
Your item 2	
Your item 3	

Once you have come up with a next action for each item, either do it right away or schedule it in your calendar.

Section 5: Being realistic about time available for tasks

If you answered Yes to Question 5A then there are two likely reasons why this is often a problem for you: either you under-estimate how much time you will have available to you and the second is that you under-estimate the time or complexity of the tasks themselves.

How many times have we thought to ourselves that we have lots of time for a big task only for the weeks to fly past with little accomplished? When we look at the time stretching ahead of us we may forget about the fact there are weekends, public holidays and possibly vacations between us and the deadline date. Then there is all additional work which will be allocated to us before the deadline, all the regular tasks which we have to do, meetings we have to attend, etc. Let's say we have a report due in seven days' time – when we have taken account of all the time which has already been taken from us over the next week, all the possible contingencies and the weekend we find we only have a few hours left to write it.

To find out exactly how much time we have left to do a task we could use Neil Fiore's (2007) tool the 'unschedule'. This tool turns the principle of scheduling on its head. The point of the unschedule is to take away all the time you *don't* have available for working on a task. It is especially useful for people who let their work spill over and intrude on their leisure time and time with their family. The unschedule works as part of a daily/weekly calendar. You can either use a very large paper diary with hourly slots or an electronic calendar such as Outlook. You schedule in all the commitments which you have such as attending meetings, visiting service users, lunch, doctor or dentist appointments. Fiore also recommends that you schedule in fun activities such as going out with friends. This is important because a common reason that people procrastinate is that they start to feel resentful about the amount of time they are spending on activities such as report writing. By putting treats into our schedule we can reduce these negative feelings.

Here is an example of an Unschedule:

Table 3

Time	Activity Scheduled	Notes
07.00–08.00	Get washed and dressed	
08.00–09.00	Take kids to school and get to work	
10.00–11.00	Team meeting	
11.00–12.00	Service user visit	
12.00–13.00		This time could be used for working on report that is due

(Continued)

Table 3   *(Continued)*

Time	Activity Scheduled	Notes
13.00–14.00	Lunch and pick up prescription	
14.00–15.00	Service user visit	
15.00–16.00		This time could be used for working on report that is due
16.00–17.00	Catch up with emails	
17.00–18.00	Travel home and pick up shopping	
18.00–19.00	Family meal	
19.00–20.00	Do dishes, phone mum and tell kids a story	
20.00–21.00		This time could be used for working on an assignment for a course which work has sent me on
21.00–22.00	Chill out with partner	
22.00–23.00	Get ready for bed	

As you can see, we might have convinced ourselves that we had lots of time in the day to do the report that we have to finish and lots of time in the evening to work on an assignment for the course we are doing. However, the reality is that we only have two hours for the report and one hour for the assignment. The positive thing is that having identified these slots we can resolve to ensure that we actually use them for achieving these goals.

Sometimes we can fall behind schedule with a large piece of work because we underestimate just how much work or how many stages the task or project involves. Writing a report about a new service user or family may require several meetings to gather all the necessary information. You will also need a further meeting to apprise your service user of what you have said about them and check that they feel that you have fairly represented their situation and their views about it. By breaking the task down into its component parts we can see exactly what has to be done, when and in what order. It is often best with this approach to start at the end product and work back through the stages. We will look at an example of how you can do this in the next section.

Problems of co-ordinating with others

If you are writing a report or planning to hold a case conference you may also need information and views from other professionals who are working with the service user. If you answered Yes to question 5B then it may be that you are frequently underestimating the difficulties in getting contributions from others. Some colleagues need several reminders to provide reports or written responses. Sometimes you may find that colleagues are going on holiday for part of the period in which you are writing your report. For these reasons it is important that you contact anyone who is to contribute to your report or project *as soon as you realise* that their contribution is needed. You should also set up a reminder in your calendar for when you expect to have heard from them so that you can progress chase if necessary.

The table below illustrates how you can work back from a final goal to schedule different elements of a job.

As you can see there are lots of stages to getting to the end of a single piece of work. By working backwards from the end product you can work out a schedule for doing the different stages which will ensure that you can achieve the final outcome on time.

In this section we have emphasised the importance of using reminders. A reminder in a diary or calendar is an example of what Lean management practitioners term a

Table 4

Goal or Task	Target Date	Notes
Deadline for final version of important report	Friday 30 March	A signed-for copy needs to be submitted so it must be posted the day before by special delivery.
Post off report	Thursday 29 March	This is latest date it can be posted so I want to have finished writing it a couple of days before so that I don't get faced with being unable to complete it due to an emergency.
Show report to service user	Wednesday 28 March	
Do final version of report – subject to approval by service user	Tuesday 27 March	I need to have shown the report to my team manager because it is the first time I have written this type of report. She may want me to do corrections. I have to give her enough time to read it because she is very busy.
Give draft report to team manager	Friday 23 March	I need to do the report over several days because it will be complex and I may end up being very busy while I am doing it.
Write report	Write over 20 March to 22 March	I need to ensure that I have got in all the information I need from other professionals who have to contribute to the report and that I have all the information I need.
Check all information has been gathered	19 March	Chase up any colleagues who need to supply information to the report but who have not submitted it. Check that I have gathered everything I need.
Visit service user to gather information for report	16 March	Need to send out visit request with plenty of notice in case date or time suggested is not suitable.
Contact any colleagues who are also making contributions to the report	12 March	
Read over existing departmental case records		
Send out appointment letter to service user		

kanban. This is a Japanese word for signal and it is a way of managing your work in such a way as to ensure that everything that needs to happen occurs on time. We will look at Lean principles more closely later in the chapter.

Section 6: Avoiding procrastination and making time for important tasks

Avoiding procrastination

If you answered Yes to question 6A then you may have a problem with procrastinating.

This may not be a generalised problem. It might be that you find it easy to get to grips with most elements of your job, yet struggle to make progress on certain tasks.

Burka and Yuen (2008) stated that it is important for people to understand why they procrastinate. They stated that procrastination has a defensive psychological function for many people and understanding the benefits which procrastination has for them is essential to finding a way to stop the behaviour. They pointed to an equation which proposed that most people believe that self-worth = ability + effort. With plenty of time available then, the limiting factor for performance will be the extent of our ability. However, if we don't give ourselves enough time to do the task properly then we don't have to face up to the limits of our ability. They suggest that if someone is a perfectionist then they will be operating on the false belief that there is only one acceptable way to do a job – the perfect way. By not starting the task on time the perfectionist is able to give themselves an excuse for not having done a perfect job. Burka and Yuen point out that people who do achieve a lot are not perfectionists but people who realise that they will often perform less than perfectly due to a number of factors, but will try to do their best anyway. Perfectionism can be dealt with by accepting that it is possible to do a job that is 'good enough'.

Another possible reason for procrastination is lack of confidence. It may be that you feel a lack of confidence around certain difficult, complex or unfamiliar tasks and this can lead to an avoidance of getting started on these tasks. This can especially be a problem with a large piece of written work such as a report. In these situations it is always best to actually make a start and write something even if you think it is not very good just so that you can feel that you have made some progress. By making tentative steps we can often find that the task is not as daunting as we thought it might be. We can also identify which elements of the task we are most in need of help with and thereby seek the appropriate assistance.

Burks and Yuen suggest that some people in management roles avoid tackling the most responsible parts of their job because it will put them in the spotlight and they will find the decision-making role to be a lonely place. When we are approaching a progression point in our job we may procrastinate in moving past that point in order to maintain the security of being in a protected position in which we are receiving mentoring or a reduced workload. For others, procrastination may be related to fears of other people beginning to have expectations of them and making greater demands as a result of them having shown themselves to be competent.

For some others, procrastination can be a form of rebellion or a vehicle for expressing annoyance at their manager. This can be at an unconscious level. Other people who procrastinate may fear competitive situations because they involve conflict and create winners and losers. They may not want to risk showing up other people's poor performance or appearing to be competitive.

Burka and Yuen suggest a regime for procrastinators which would fit well with a cognitive behavioural approach. Having developed an understanding of why you procrastinate they suggest that you identify the excuses you may have for delaying starting or progressing projects. They also suggest that you identify the behaviours which you commonly perform instead of the task you were supposed to be doing. They then suggest that you pick a single feasible goal in relation to what you procrastinate with and work on that for the next two weeks. They suggest that it should be the smallest goal which you could aim towards that would demonstrate to you that you were capable of changing your behaviour. They say that you should aim to work on your goal for short periods of time and stick to that amount of time regardless of the quality of work you have attained in that time. You should work on the project regardless of whether you are feeling motivated at the time you start. You should also not worry about whether the work you are producing is perfect or not. You should revise the goal if it turns out to be unrealistic or unexpected genuine obstacles get in the way.

The table below gives a format for exploring why you procrastinate.

Table 5

Task which I procrastinate with	Reasons I might procrastinate with this task	Behaviours which I carry out instead of the task I am avoiding	Function which the procrastination achieves	Benefit of stopping procrastinating
Making appointments with new service users	I am afraid that my new service user will think I am a 'phony' who is not competent to help them or that I will be overwhelmed by the scope of the problems they need help with	Reading files and doing admin	Prevents me from facing up to the fact that I am not a completely perfect social worker and I think that you have to be perfect to make the grade	I can start work with new service users more quickly and have more time to build up a constructive relationship. I can also try to accept that I might be a 'good enough' social worker who is nevertheless growing into a better social worker

Achievable behavioural change I will try to make:

The next time I get a referral I will send out an appointment the same day as I get the referral. I will do this with every new referral for the next month.

The principle of Burk and Yuen's approach is that by making small changes and accomplishing small goals you can re-educate yourself about what you are capable of and establish a new self-identity of someone who can grasp difficult tasks and get them done.

Having energy for important tasks

If you answered Yes to question 6B then you may be having problems because you are prioritising routine tasks at the expense of having energy for bigger projects.

Lange (2011) described the habits of author Ian Fleming, creator of James Bond. After breakfast and a swim in the Caribbean Sea, Fleming would start work in his Jamaican home at 09.00. He would stop at noon – go for another swim and sunbathe and then have lunch and have a short sleep in the late afternoon. He would do some more work from 17.00–18.30, looking over his work from earlier in the day and doing corrections. He would then finish, get himself a drink and forget about his work for the rest of the day. Few of us have the luxury of being able to work from a home in the Caribbean or work as few hours as Fleming did. However, there are some lessons we can learn from him. First is the benefit of having a regular routine. Fleming trained himself to have the discipline of having a regular focused time for doing his work. Second, we can learn the value of doing important complex work at a time in the day when we are rested and our brain is refreshed and energised. Physical activity and rest were programmed into Fleming's day and he tackled his important work at a time when he had most energy.

Most us of course will have lots of mundane tasks and admin, which Fleming did not have to bother with. However, we will have times of the day in which our powers of thinking and concentration are at their peak. Suppose we come in and deal first with lots of routine tasks such as non-urgent email and phone calls, then go out on social work visits and then try to engage with a large complex piece of work like a report in the last two hours of the day. With this strategy we are dealing with increasingly complex tasks as the day goes on. By the time we get round to starting our difficult report we are likely to be tired and lacking the energy required to do it. If we have a complex and demanding task then we should ideally plan to start it when we are freshest. For most people this is likely to be a couple of hours after we wake up.

A similar principle applies to jobs we are not looking forward to. Lord Lew Grade, a British TV and movie mogul of the 1960s and 70s would famously schedule difficult meetings with his producers for 07.30 or earlier. By getting our most difficult task out of the way first thing we can look forward to enjoying the rest of the day rather than continually feeling anxiety or irritation about the task which is hanging over us. Furthermore, completing a difficult task first is energising and may raise our optimism about what else we can achieve over the course of the day.

Section 7: Meetings

If you answered yes to question 7A then you may be experiencing frustration at spending long periods of time in long and unfocused meetings. If you are a field social worker you may not have much control over the meetings you attend. However, there may be opportunities to 'diplomatically' make suggestions for how a regularly occurring meeting can be run or you may sometimes find yourself in the position of Chair. Meetings which I chair are always as short as possible and run to time.

Here are some tips for running effective meetings.

1. Ensure that the people who are invited are at the correct operational or strategic level for the issues under discussion. People who just need to be aware of decisions can be sent the outcomes of the meeting electronically. If it is important to invite someone solely for etiquette or political reasons then invite them in a way which leaves it open for them to politely refuse the invitation. Always try to keep membership of meetings as small as possible to achieve the objectives.

2. Try to avoid scheduling meetings for longer than 75 minutes. This is a good running time because it allows the meeting to **exceptionally** run to 90 minutes without disrupting people's schedules. At 60 minutes you should be drawing the meeting to a close. If you need a much longer meeting then it usually means that there are tasks which would be better done outside of the meeting by a task and finish group made up of a subset of members of the meeting.

3. Have an agenda drawn up before the meeting. Give participants an opportunity to put items on the agenda by email in advance of the meeting. At the beginning of the meeting ask if anyone has any additional items to add to the agenda. Only allow them to be added if there is space or they are urgent. Otherwise add them to the agenda for the next meeting. Don't ask people if they have 'any other business' once the agenda has been exhausted. This may encourage people to raise issues for the sake of it. The exception to this is meetings which directly concern the planning of care for a service user. In those sorts of meetings it is important that participants are given the chance to raise any additional concerns. Service users should always be given additional opportunities to speak. If the meeting finishes early then that is a good chance for people to network informally over a coffee or leave early for their next engagement.

4. Keep professionals to subject and do not allow the meeting to stray onto issues which are not within its remit. Have in advance an estimate of how much time each item on the agenda is likely to occupy and keep the meeting running to time.

5. Always close the meeting with thanks to the attendees and details of date and location of next meeting. Ensure that everyone is clear about the decisions which have been made and who is responsible for any actions.

Often there are decisions made at meetings which people who were not present have to be aware of or actions which need to taken before the next meeting. It is therefore more important that meeting notes come out quickly and are accurate than that they provide an exhaustive account of what was discussed in the meeting.

Long minutes which record long discussions are not very useful and take a long time to write. They are not often a genuine records of discussions in any case as people will frequently say, 'This is not for minuting'.

A way of recording meetings, and one which fits with Lean principles, is simply to record decisions and action points. I would suggest producing a record of meetings in a table with four column headings: Subject discussed, Decisions taken, Actions required and Name(s) of person(s) responsible for actions. If the information is recorded in this way, it can be shared and agreed by those present before the close of the meeting and emailed out to all those present and anyone additional on the circulation list within an hour of the meeting closing. This ensures that information is circulated quickly, effectively and accurately with no additional work for the note taker and no need to dishonestly represent the discussion. Always check that the format you use is in accordance with agency policies.

An example is illustrated below:

Table 6

Notes of Team Meeting Held on 31 January

Subject discussed	Decision taken	Person responsible
1. Discussions in the interview room next to reception can be heard by people in waiting room.	Office manager to be asked to look into soundproofing measures for this interview room.	Team manager to contact office manager.
2.		
3.		
4.		

Section 8: Managing your expectations of what you will achieve with your time

If you answered Yes to question 8 then you may be burdening yourself with over-excessive expectations. This is related to the earlier point about under-estimating how much work is involved in getting tasks done, though the costs here are emotional rather than in terms of what is achieved.

Go back to the end of Chapter 1 and look at the I Did exercise. If you haven't already tried this exercise then you might want to try it now. You may be pleasantly surprised at just how much you have achieved.

Section 9: Making use of found time

A number of years ago I did a second bachelor's degree as a part-time student. Much of my reading and studying for the degree was done on my daily train commute.

The journey was an hour each way, and British trains being what they are I frequently had extra time from delays and time spent waiting in stations. Obviously if you commute to work by car then you cannot use your time in this way. However, all of us will have time away from our desk when we have to wait for something or somebody. It might be waiting in line for coffee, or sitting in a waiting room for a meeting to start or time between appointments. If we have an electronic device such as a smartphone then we can use this time to answer simple emails or read useful news items on sites such as *Community Care*. If you don't have an electronic device then take a book or a document which is useful to your work and a notepad. You can use your notepad to jot down comments which you want to raise at the meeting. If you are part of a committee then you can use this time to read the papers for your upcoming meeting.

Most of us have short blocks of useful time which arise over the course of the day. By being prepared with things to read or short tasks to do you can optimise that time. If you can find 45 minutes in an average 7.4-hour day then you can boost your productivity by 10 per cent. You will never need to feel frustrated or annoyed about a delay again – you just transform it into productive time.

Section 10: Adopting a Lean approach to work

Question 10 asked you about whether you had an active approach to identifying how efficient you are in your work life. There are more or less efficient ways of doing things in all aspects of our life. An efficient way of going round a supermarket would be to buy items which are shelved together at the same time rather than picking up items in the order they appear on the shopping list. We would take a few moments to plan our route round the supermarket so that we would not have to go backwards and forwards across the store repeatedly. If we wanted to be effective as well as efficient we would pick up frozen items last to avoid them defrosting. We can adopt similar principles to social work by trying to group together home visits in the same locality. If we are going to be putting the same information into several places at around the same time, such as case notes and reports, then we can save time by writing the information once in the most detailed format that is needed and then editing it down to suit the other formats in which it is needed.

We all have strategies for saving time and energy but we may not do this in a systematic way. Lean is a method for systematically identifying wasted effort and inefficient and ineffective processes. We will look at how Lean principles can be used in an organisational context in a later chapter but here I will introduce the concept from the point of view of the individual worker.

Lean is a method for improving the efficiency of workplaces and getting greater productivity from workers. Lean is normally carried out at an organisational level, and we will be dealing with this in a later chapter. However, a Lean approach to work is also something which individual workers can apply to their own personal work. In many ways Lean thinking is more a discipline or a way of being than just a method of improving workplace efficiency. Lean working is arguably mindful working and the association with eastern spiritual disciplines is reflected in the awarding of different coloured belts to denote the level of expertise in Lean practitioners.

Lean developed originally as an improvement process by the Toyota motor company (Black and Miller, 2008). Kiichiro Toyoda, son of Toyota founder Sakichi Toyoda, visited the USA in the 1930s to study the production methods of the Ford Motor company. However, he also visited American supermarkets. He was impressed at the methods which were used to make the supermarkets work efficiently. An effective supermarket has to hold just the right amount of stock and no more while ensuring that it does not run out of stock of any of its products. Lean improves on the production line system by looking at product flow and identifying bottlenecks and other forms of waste in systems.

At this point you may be asking the question of what this type of industrial process has to do with a profession like social work which is all about listening to people and helping them. The answer is nothing in relation to the parts of social work which are about our relationships with service users. However, it does have a lot to offer to the other parts of the job. As I mentioned at the beginning of this chapter it is frequently claimed that social workers spend more time on admin than at any time in the past. If it is true that social workers are spending a disproportionately high amount of time on admin then we should be investing time and energy on fixing this. It is important to note that not all work that comes into the category of admin and recording is routine or unskilled. Tasks such as case recording and sharing information with colleagues are concerned with decision making and are therefore crucial components of the job even though they are not the best loved. They are elements of the job which we need to perform effectively as well as more efficiently.

Staats and Upton (2011) stated that Lean principles can be applied to tasks which involve judgement and expertise just as readily as they can to routine processes.

I will look at four of the six key areas which Staats and Upton identified and look in turn at how each could be applied to social work.

1. Continually rooting out waste should be an integral part of every knowledge worker's job

Staats and Upton argued that we should constantly be asking ourselves questions such as, 'Why am I attending this meeting? Why am I writing this report? Why am I standing at the printer?' Of course we will be doing these things for a reason. However, if we get to the root reason or fundamental purpose of why we are doing them then we might conclude that there is an easier or more cost-effective way of achieving the same outcome. A technique for doing this in Lean is called the Five Whys. This involves asking the question Why? in relation to something which we are doing. The question Why? is then asked again repeatedly until we get to the root reason of why something is really being done. To give an example of this let's look at the last sample question in my list above:

Why are you standing at the printer?

I am printing off copies of the latest report on a service user for a case conference.

Why?

So that all the participants in the case conference have a copy.

Why?

So that they all have the most up-to-date information about the service user.

Why?

So that they can contribute meaningfully to the case conference about the service user and help plan a way forward for the service user.

We only asked four Whys this time but I think we got to the core reason for the task.

Once we have drilled down to why we are performing the task we can identify that it is both wasteful and ineffective. In this example the meeting which we are doing the printing/photocopying for is not there for people to spend time wading through papers – it is there to plan a way forward for the service user. A more effective way forward would therefore be to email the report to the participants in advance of the meeting and ask them to read it and come prepared with ideas about how they or their agency could contribute to a care plan. If any of the participants feel that they will need a paper copy of the report at the meeting then they can print it off in their own time and at their expense. With this new process you as the report writer have saved a lot of time on printing/copying. However, the really important benefit of this alternative approach is in terms of the meeting becoming more productive. There will be no need to spend large amounts of time in the meeting reading the report. Furthermore, participants will hopefully have come to the meeting with some suggestions for supporting the service user already formulated. Some participants may also have checked on the availability of resources to support their suggestions – saving an additional delay while availability of resources is checked. The majority of the meeting can therefore be used for planning a realistic strategy.

Sometimes we even come to question whether a particular procedure is actually needed. When I worked as a mental health team manager, social workers were being asked to complete long reports on people being referred for residential drug or alcohol rehabilitation. The reason given was to assess whether it was appropriate to finance this costly service and to provide background information for the agency that would work with the service user. After a year I found that 100 per cent of referrals for residential rehabilitation had been approved. Furthermore, the agencies themselves were doing extensive reports on their new referrals. Thus the report that social workers were doing was neither useful for the agencies providing the care nor for gatekeeping resources. It was a complete waste of expensive social worker time and energy. It could be replaced by a much simpler and more streamlined process for agreeing funding.

In a Lean organisation workers and managers at all levels will be constantly thinking about how waste can be eliminated from what they do.

Exercise

Five Whys

Consider a task you have to do in your work which you think is unduly time consuming or not appropriate to your job role. Use the Five Whys to find out the fundamental purpose of the task, then come up with a more Lean way of achieving the same goal.

Table 7

Procedure:
Why:
Why:
Why:
Why:
Why:
Lean alternative way of achieving purpose of the time-consuming activity:
Any steps I may need to take to change the procedure to make it less time consuming (this step may be necessary where you need permissions, additional resources or the cooperation of others to change how a particular activity is carried out):

2. Strive to make tacit knowledge explicit

This is concerned with specifying how a task should be performed and in what timescales and other criteria. This is something which social services departments are usually good at. There is sometimes resistance from social workers to having their job specified in this way and some object to the time limits being set on assessments for example. However, by specifying tasks we can bring in elements of quality assurance and ensure that processes such as assessment are doing what they intended to achieve and within the timescale required.

3. Specify how communication should take place

Serious case reviews and similar reports regularly come out with the recommendation that communication between different workers and agencies should be improved. Often that is taken to mean more communication. However, most of us are already overwhelmed with emails and other forms of communication. Effective communication has to be timely, effective and targeted. The recipient also has to be aware of the significance of the communication. For example, if we are told that a service user's partner has left him then this might be just background information. However, if previous occasions of the partner leaving have led to an act of self-harm or a deterioration of mental health then this information is extremely significant. A good risk assessment model and effective multi-disciplinary working should ensure that information is communicated in a way that is meaningful. It is important therefore that workers all understand each other's professional culture and type of language which they use to express different types of concern. They also need to have a shared understanding of the cases which they are working on, the nature of each other's role and the channels to be used for communicating serious concerns.

A Lean approach to communication will ensure that communication is timely, accurate and effective.

4. Address problems quickly and directly

This is about everyone taking responsibility for their part of their organisation, recognising where there may be problems with systems and working on solutions. People who use admin systems are much closer to them and more able to identify and articulate where they might not be functioning as they should than managers who are remote from them. The aim of the Toyota production system is to make everyone part of a 'problem solving engine'. Rather than complaining in vague terms about why case recording and admin systems (for example) are not working, social workers should think about how they can be made more effective for their needs. When it is time to change the technology, equipment or software systems being used then it is vital that social workers take an active interest in informing this process. It is only by informing technicians and administrators of what we need for doing our jobs effectively that we can ensure that we get the systems which we need. Admin and technology are the business of every professional.

Hopefully this section on managing time to improve resilience has been helpful to you in terms of thinking about how you can make your work flow more effectively.

Chapter recap

In this chapter we moved away from an explicit focus on spiritual and philosophical aspects of work which had featured in the earlier chapters. However, you probably grasped the value of mindfulness in helping us to focus on working more efficiently. Lean management which I introduced at the end of the chapter is almost a spiritual discipline with practitioners receiving different coloured belts as they achieve greater experience and competence. By developing an inner stillness and calm and decluttering our mind we can operate in a way which uses less effort to achieve greater progress.

Further reading

If you want to read more about time management I would thoroughly recommend reading David Allen's books *Getting Things Done* and the follow-up *Making It All Work*.

For a basic introduction to the concepts of Lean management there are lots of short videos on YouTube – though be warned that some take the relationship with Japanese martial arts a little too seriously and dress up in judo outfits for their presentations. If you want to further explore Lean management then there are lots of books on the topic but *Lean for the Public Sector* by Bert Teeuwen is particularly useful for anyone in the public sector.

If procrastination is a serious problem for you then I would highly recommend buying Burka and Yuen's book *Procrastination: Why you do it, what to do about it now*. It is a marvellous resource which fully explores the psychology of procrastination. It starts from the important perspective that dysfunctional behaviours have a function and that it is only by reaching an understanding of the purpose which they serve for us that we can get free from them.

Next up!

In the next chapter we are going to look at the importance of new technology to social work and how it can be used to help us to operationalise some of the time-saving tips I have introduced in this chapter. We will also consider the barriers to introducing new technology to social work. New models of employing social workers and structuring services will be considered and we will look at the benefits and disadvantages of these alternative models.

5

MAKING EFFECTIVE USE OF NEW TECHNOLOGY AND NEW WORK STYLES TO ENHANCE PRACTICE

Key Concepts and Issues in this Chapter

- Applying new technologies to public sector work and the cultural barriers to its effective implementation
- Using new technology to make case recording, scheduling and report writing easier
- Preventing digital technologies from distracting our attention, dominating our work and damaging our work/life balance
- Using social media safely
- Effective deployment of hot desking and agile working
- Social work practices and other changes to how social work services are provided

---

Digital innovation and social work

If I asked you to come up with names of some people who were pioneers of digital technology I imagine you would give me a list of names such as Steve Jobs, Mark Zuckerberg, Bill Gates or going back in history Alan Turing. The odds are that your list would all be men. My digital hero is a woman and you probably have not heard of her. Her name is Grace Hopper, she was a Rear Admiral in the U.S. Navy and she was born in 1906 and died in 1992. Among her accomplishments was being a programmer of the 16-metre long Harvard Mark 1 computer during the Second World War, inventing the very first compiler program and many, many other innovations in computer technology over a very long career. One of her more amusing contributions was to coin 'debugging' a computer after an incident in which she removed a moth in a computer relay. In 1973 she was the first woman to be made a Distinguished Fellow of the British Computer Society. In 1986 at her (involuntary) retirement she was awarded the Defense Distinguished Service medal. These are just a few of the accolades and awards which this amazing woman won over her career.

The reason I think Grace has much to teach us in social work is because of her positive attitude towards risk taking and striving for improvement and her ability to see clearly all the practical benefits which technology can bring. Unfortunately many social workers operate within very risk-averse organisational cultures where the first response to any new technology is to list all the potential snags and then decide it is too risky to be used. I remember a time when many social workers were denied access to the internet at work in case they spent their time playing poker or looking for cheap holidays. Nowadays that attitude would seem ridiculous. However, just as social workers were once denied access to the powerful tool of the internet, employers are currently taking risk-averse approaches to new technologies which would allow social workers to use their time more effectively. By contrast, Grace Hopper always encouraged young people whom she trained to take risks and was willing to back them up. One of the many quotes of wisdom attributed to her was, 'If it's a good idea, go ahead and do it. It is much easier to apologise than it is to get permission' (quoted in Purrington et al., 2003). This is an especially useful motto for anyone working in a bureaucracy, though do bear in mind that you can get disciplined if your idea breaches local authority policy.

Importantly, Grace Hopper was always in favour of innovation and progress. She said that 'People love to say "we've always done it this way". I try to fight that. That's why I have a clock on my wall that runs counter-clockwise' (quoted in Schieber, 1987). In the 1980s Hopper recognised that paper was becoming redundant and that records which were then on paper could be stored electronically. Hopper made this observation in the 1986 issue of a Navy magazine. This was thirty years ago and yet I know social workers today who are still writing case notes and reports on notepads and passing the notes to a typing pool. In one authority in England staff were recently given state of the art tablets. The idea was that workers would be able to put information directly onto case notes while on visits as well as completing important forms while on visits. This is important both from the point of view of saving worker time and also ensuring that case notes are always completely up to date. The innovative policy was scuppered by the authority's IT department who refused to allow this direct linkage to authority information systems – presumably because of security fears. Of course, security is an important issue but there should be ways of building in improved security to overcome these risks. As a result of the IT department's intransigence the state of the art tablets are going to be used as expensive notepads. Buying good IT and properly securing it is expensive but the cost savings associated with greater efficiency make it a very effective investment.

Using technology effectively

Grace Hopper showed that innovation is not restricted to the private sector and that with courage and imagination, technological innovation can be driven ahead in the public sector. The local government sector desperately needs its own Grace. While we are waiting for one to appear there are still lots of opportunities to make the best use of the technology we are provided with.

Electronic calendars

These are very effective ways of planning our use of time. In the last chapter we looked at how techniques such as creating an unschedule and putting entries into our calendar for important tasks from our to-do list. An electronic calendar such as Outlook provides a good mechanism for this as it is easy to attach notes to the entries and a lot easier to change or delete items as contingencies arise.

The other benefit of an electronic calendar is that if you are inviting colleagues to a meeting then you can send them an invitation through the scheduling facility in Outlook. All your invitees need to do is to click 'accept' on your meeting request and the meeting will go into their calendar without them having to type in anything. If you have a Blackberry or other mobile device then you can schedule appointments with service users when you are out on visits. If you have an iPad or other tablet device, then even if it is not connected to the internet you can still enter appointments into your Outlook calendar and then they should be uploaded into the system as soon as you get into a wi-fi area. If you are not issued with equipment such as this you can of course buy your own mobile or tablet device. If you are going to use the equipment for work you will have to get permission from your employer and have a safety check on it. This ought to be welcomed by your employer but I have heard of local authorities preventing their workers from linking work email accounts and calendars to their own devices. This is a very short-sighted policy but sadly all too typical of the sector.

Some social workers run two diaries – an electronic one and a paper one. This is, however, a recipe for confusion and it prevents you from leveraging the benefits of electronic scheduling.

Using digital record keeping to minimise time spent on administration tasks

As I have indicated above, the best way to streamline your recording and minimise your workload is to have devices which can interface directly with all the databases and systems which you are required to work with. Ideally, these systems should talk to each other so that you only ever have to record a piece of information once and it then goes to every other place that that information is needed. This requires good information systems design and is a reason why managers and frontline workers should take an active interest in the computer systems of their agencies. If you are ever offered the opportunity to be part of a committee in your organisation which is concerned with purchase or implementation of a new system for recording and managing data then you should take it. It is only by successfully communicating the needs of frontline workers that you can ensure that information systems do what we need them to do. You will have to use any IT system that your authority buys for a number of years, so any help you give in specifying it will reap dividends to you and your colleagues.

While few authorities will offer you the type of functionality and connectivity I am suggesting above, many will at least now offer you an iPad or other tablet device. You can record information which the service user gives to you in draft form. Facts which are to go into reports can be checked through with the service user before leaving the visit. Then as soon as possible after the visit this information can be tidied up, made grammatically correct and expanded upon to fit the format needed for reports and case notes, etc. Nobody in this day and age should be writing information in a notepad and then retyping their words into a computer or writing it out again neatly for a typist. These practices are hugely inefficient and are one of the reasons for reports in the social work media that social workers are spending large amounts of their time doing admin. Used correctly, digital devices can reduce our workload considerably. I wrote most of this book on a laptop. Some of it was drafted on an iPad in trains and hotel rooms, sent to myself by email and then cut and pasted into my draft manuscript. No pens have been used in the creation of this book other than to sign the contract with the publisher. If you do possess a pen then please consider throwing it away now and learning the discipline of doing all your writing electronically. I know that some people claim that they cannot think as clearly when in front of a keyboard as they can on paper. However, you will find that this is probably just because it is what you are familiar with and that typing information will become natural to you once you get more practice.

Mobile phones

All social workers should get a mobile phone so that they can easily ask for help if they become stranded or they run into difficulties. Ideally this should be a smartphone with email.

Wrangling your email inbox

Although technology can reduce stress through efficiency, email is a technology which has been found to create a great deal of stress for workers. In fact, some people feel that they could spend all their time trying to empty their email inbox. This can drive their whole time in the office. Unfortunately email is such a cost-free form of communication (for the sender) that people will send queries by email which they would not bother asking if they had to make a phone call or walk down a corridor. Emails also make it possible to send the same email to multiple recipients, which often include large numbers of people for whom the email contents are irrelevant. What many people fail to realise is that this seemingly 'free' form of communication carries a significant cost to the recipient. There is the time taken to read the email; the time taken to think about whether the email is relevant to us; the time to compose and write a response (if one is required); the time taken to note down any important information in the email or save any attached documents; and then the time taken to resume our other work or move onto our next task following time spent on our inbox. Jackson et al. (2006) worked out a formula for calculating the cost to an organisation of its employees reading emails.

Organisational cost of reading email = $(t1+t2)wn$

Where t1 is the time taken to read all of a batch of emails received in minutes, t2 = the time taken to recover and move on to next task, w = the average cost per minute of employing staff and n is the number of people in the organisation. Think about your email inbox for a moment and then think of the time costs of it multiplied by the number of colleagues in your agency.

Jackson et al. found in their study of a UK business that 16 per cent of emails were copied in to people unnecessarily, 13 per cent were irrelevant to the recipient or untargeted, and only 46 per cent of emails which required a response made the action required explicit.

Email is therefore not free at all. There is a cost in worker time imposed on the recipients of every email. We can help reduce these costs by:

1. Avoiding sending out emails to everyone in our organisation or large groups of people when the email could be more targeted. That is a small amount of extra time for us but it is a big saving to all the people who don't receive unnecessary communications.
2. Making it clear in the subject line exactly what the topic is, whether the email is urgent and whether it is for information or for action.
3. Where actions are required, making these explicit and who is responsible for which actions.

I think that organisations should seriously consider levying internal costs on departments for the volume of email traffic which they generate. I am not aware of this approach having been used. However, some organisations set aside days in which emails cannot be sent. Others have experimented with the use of Facebook-style groups as an alternative to email for sharing information and encouraging collaboration between different parts of agencies.

In the absence of better agency policies we can help reduce the negative effects of emails on ourselves by developing good email habits.

I would recommend avoiding answering emails on a Monday morning unless they appear urgent. This is the time that people are most likely to be at their desk and there is a significant chance that they will respond to your email right away with a follow-up query. It is possible to spend a Monday morning working on emails and have more emails in your inbox by lunchtime than you started with. I would recommend answering emails at the end of the day when your energy levels for large pieces of work are at their lowest and there is less chances of getting further responses to your inbox.

Not everything in your email inbox needs to be treated in the same way. Queries and emails that require actions that can be completed very quickly (i.e. less than five minutes' work each) are best dealt with right away and then deleted or archived. Emails which all relate to a similar topic, and you intend to deal with them at the same time, should be put together in a folder and a time for dealing with them scheduled in your calendar. For example, if you have sent out a lot of invitations to a meeting and you plan to send out venue details and an agenda once you have all your replies in, then put all the replies into one clearly labelled folder (e.g. case conference meeting responses) as they arrive. This allows you to quickly assess who is coming once all the replies are in rather than having to trawl through your whole inbox. The same approach can be used if you have a number of emails which require short to moderate pieces of work that you don't have enough time for at the moment. You could put them in a folder named admin tasks and then schedule time in a day in which you have time in the office to do them. It is important not to have too many folders at once and also to clear them out or delete them regularly. Emails which request a report or a large piece of work should be turned into a task in Outlook with a deadline for completion put into your calendar system. Blocks of time should be allocated for completing the task and a reminder set up to ensure that you are on track with working towards completion.

If you subscribe to emails which are about updates in your field, e.g. emails from *Community Care* or the *Guardian* about social work news, these can be put in a folder. If you have email on a smartphone you can read these emails while queuing for coffee, waiting for an elevator, etc.

Exercise

Reviewing Your Use of Email

Over a period of a week record how much time you are spending on emails and what time of day you are working on them. For each email session make a brief record of the degree to which the time was used effectively and whether there are any changes which you could make to your use of email which could have made the use of time more effective. Also reflect on the emails which you write yourself and consider whether another form of communication such as phoning might have been more effective. Also consider whether use of folders could make it easier for you to find emails which you need.

At the end of the week come up with a strategy for using your email inbox more effectively and start implementing it the following week.

Getting breaks from technology

Rosen (2015) described the phenomena of FOMO (fear of missing out) and FOBO (fear of being offline). Many people, and I have to confess that I am one of them, have developed a habit of constantly checking digital devices and looking at their emails, Twitter account, Facebook, etc. This is an addiction and it can be annoying to other people and can intrude on our personal life. Rosen recommends training yourself to have periods without accessing technology. He also suggests that it is important to keep digital devices out of the bedroom and not look at computer or phone screens an hour before going to bed because they can affect the quality of sleep. Rosen also suggests that we should have a break from working at a computer every 1.5 hours and have a 10-minute break in which we go for a walk, have some brief exercise or listen to some relaxing music. The 1.5 hour rule is apparently linked to research evidence that our brains work in 1.5 hour cycles with intermittent rest periods. Whether or not you want to stick to 1.5 hour bursts of activity, most people will find that regular rest breaks are helpful when engaged in long difficult written tasks.

Use of social media

A high percentage of the population of the UK now have Facebook accounts and will be aware of the benefits of it as a way of sharing news and experiences with family, friends and acquaintants. Many will also use resources such as Twitter and other online forums. These can be excellent ways of sharing information and ideas and having debates. However, there are dangers for social workers in relation to social media use. The first is that disgruntled service users (often people who had their children removed) will try to track down where you live and even publish photos or information about you online. It is very important if you are a social worker to understand the security settings on social media accounts. Remember also that even if you only share your postings with friends, things which you post on their accounts could be seen by a much wider audience. Photos of you and your family can be tagged with your name and the date and location of the photo for example. All sorts of information, which people assume is private, is available online and searchable such as the sale price of your house, unlisted phone numbers, etc. The internet also allows us to make connections between these different types of information. I was once puzzled by the identity of someone who had sent me a message on Twitter. I googled their Twitter name. This not only revealed their name but also links on all sorts of potentially embarrassing hook-up websites in which they used the same username.

The second danger for social workers who use social media is that people who are ill-disposed towards them, and this can include service users, unfriendly co-workers, and even bullying bosses, can scan the internet looking for material to use against them. Schraer (2015) reported on a social worker who had been reported to the Health and Care Professions Council (HCPC) by a member of the public for writing offensive tweets to David Cameron, Donald Trump and others. It is understood from reports elsewhere that the Twitter account had few followers so it is unlikely that many people actually read the offensive tweets. However, the case was taken seriously enough for the case to go before the HCPC. I have also heard anecdotally of a social worker who was reported to their employer for making rude comments to someone who had had dealings with them on Ebay.

Social work is considered to be a 'moral profession' and so any public deviation from what is considered to be that professional image can be used against you. The use of aliases and avatars will not necessarily protect you due to the inter-connectedness of the internet. Local authorities are very conservative and risk-averse organisations and professional regulatory bodies will take any allegations about your conduct from the public very seriously even if there is malicious intent behind the referral.

The British Association of Social Workers (2012b) has a very good Social Media Policy which every social worker should read carefully. I would recommend that if you post views about social work issues that you should stick to discussing these in the abstract and never refer to any work which you have actually done or been involved in yourself. This includes positive comments as well as negative ones. If you post on Facebook 'Had a really positive time working with service users this afternoon', that could be taken by someone that you didn't feel positive about whoever you saw in the morning. It is best not to discuss your work at all. When posting your views about social or political issues always ensure that you can defend your position against accusations of any kind of prejudice. If someone calls you out for being unkind, unfair or making sweeping generalisations about anything always be prepared to apologise, even if you think they have unreasonably taken offence. We can all use more friends and there is no point in making enemies.

Used properly, social media like Twitter can give you access to lots of sources of information which will be immensely useful to you in your career. You can search Twitter to look for people to follow using ordinary search terms like 'social work' and hashtags such as #socialwork which aid in searching. Twitter will also give you suggestions of who to follow based on your interests. Twitter often gives you opportunities to interact directly with writers, politicians, academics and others through commenting on their tweets. You should not expect replies from famous people but it is exciting when it does happen.

Hot desking and agile working

Hot desking means not having your own desk but instead finding a desk when you need one. Agile working is a related concept and refers to the ability to work easily in a range of environments. If you are an agile worker then if you have time between visits in which it is impractical to return to the office, you can use other locations such as cafes (provided privacy of data is ensured) or your car to catch up with recording or report writing. Never leave your computer unattended with your email or any confidential documents open or where your screen could be overlooked by others. Agile working requires good mobile IT devices such as iPads or laptops, which as I have stated before should ideally be linked to email and local authority recording systems. Hot desking just requires the ability to obtain a desk and log onto a computer in a shared office environment. Hot desking and agile working are based on the principle that in a paperless working environment we have no need of permanent desks, filing cabinets, etc. They also work on the principle that since social workers should be spending most of their time out in the field it is wasteful of resources to provide a permanent personal desk and computer for each worker. It is therefore a cost-effective strategy.

There are also positive benefits for social workers themselves in hot desking. We tend in a normal office environment to spend all our time with the same colleagues. Hot desking can give us the opportunity to randomly mix with colleagues from other teams or even other professions.

Personally I believe that hot desking and agile working have a lot of benefits for social work but the experiences of many social workers have not been good. McGregor (2012a) reported on a survey undertaken by *Community Care* and Unison on social worker experience of hot desking. A large percentage of respondents felt that they had not been properly equipped and supported. Nine out of ten people in the survey had commented that hot desking had a negative effect on morale and that they had less access to peer support. Social workers sometimes need quiet and privacy for sensitive phone calls. They also need space to have supportive conversations with colleagues. The large open-plan offices often associated with hot desking do not facilitate these important interactions. Many local authorities have adopted this approach to save money but have not thought about alternative ways to provide some of the important functions of a conventional environment. To leverage the benefits of hot desking thought needs to be put into the design of the office environment. It cannot all be about cost cutting.

Small changes on the part of workers and managers can make a difference to the experience of workers who are hot desking. Bee (2015) mentioned the importance of workers not locking up computers which were supposed to be for communal use. He also suggests the use of software to track the availability of free workstations so that social workers can easily discover where the nearest free workstation is to them.

Fayard and Weeks (2011) discussed how workspace can be designed to facilitate collaboration between workers while allowing them the privacy they needed. They observed that a number of studies have shown that when employees are in large open-plan offices they often have much more superficial discussions because they are aware that other people can hear them. They suggest that offices need to have spaces where people can meet accidentally such as corridors but the architecture needs to also include features such as alcoves in which people can have privacy to continue the conversations which they strike up with colleagues. Areas can be created which have a mixed function, e.g. sofas to sit and have discussions on and printers/copiers in the same area. The sharing of social and work space makes workers feel less self-conscious about sitting and having a discussion than they might if there was no office equipment in the area. They also said that management has an important role in promoting collaboration by not making derogatory remarks whether in jest or otherwise to workers who are having discussions in social areas. Instituting modern work practices is only going to be effective when the professional needs of social workers are taken into account in how they are implemented.

Understanding changes in how social care is structured: outsourcing, privatisation and markets

The structure of public services continues to change at a rapid rate. The traditional employers of social workers, local authorities, are increasingly becoming purchasers of services rather than service providers. This process began with the contracting out of services such as residential care and is increasingly being applied to qualified social work roles. Jones (2015) described the moves towards outsourcing child protection services. There is a great deal of negativity towards outsourcing in the social work sector. While understanding these concerns I also consider that the profession should recognise that these changes offer opportunities to social workers to have greater control over how their services operate.

The use of markets and a move towards privatising public services began during the government of UK Prime Minister Mrs Thatcher. This pattern has continued through subsequent UK governments and has spread internationally. More recently, the country of Greece has been asked to open up its public services to privatisation as a condition of receiving international bailout money. These trends parallel a growing use of outsourcing in the private sector. The advantages of outsourcing parts of an organisation's activities are that the customer organisation does not need to make capital investment in the activity and that it can make full use of specialist expertise which exists in the market. The negative side of the equation is that it is less easy for government to regulate the quality of outsourced services.

The application of markets and quasi-markets within public services also has the purpose of forcing service departments to improve their performance in meeting the needs of their internal 'customers' through making them compete with rival departments in other organisations. A few years ago I co-facilitated a team-building exercise for a hospital laboratory. The turnaround for certain types of lab results had previously been a week but in order to win a contract the lab managed to reduce that turnaround time drastically. The problem had not been lack of resources but just a lack of identification of bottlenecks, which were slowing down processing.

The potential benefit of competition for providing public services is greater performance but the downside is the cost of failing departments which fail to win contracts.

Outsourcing forces public bodies to acknowledge the real cost of certain activities. For example, if the writing of certain types of report is outsourced and the organisation is charged per report then it causes managers to think more carefully about whether all the reports they are asking for are actually required.

However, there are costs and dangers associated with privatisation of social services. In 2011 the field of older people's care was rocked by a scandal of the collapse of the care home company Southern Cross. This was caused by the owners of the company selling off the care home buildings to realise large profits and then renting back the residences from the new owners. The additional costs for the remaining care home business in paying the high rents became unsustainable and the company collapsed. Local authorities then had to pick up responsibility for the Southern Cross residents.

An investigation by the *Financial Times* (O'Connor and O'Murchu, 2011) in the wake of the Southern Cross scandal found much poorer Care Quality Commission (CQC) ratings for the quality of care homes in the private sector in comparison to the state and voluntary sectors. An editorial in the *Financial Times* (2011) declared the state of UK care homes to be an 'affront to human dignity'. They found that the model of privatisation for older people's care had a 'fundamental flaw'. This flaw was that competition between homes caused under-occupancy and squeezes in funding led private companies to cut back on the quality of care to boost profits. When these factors are combined with the psychological costs to frail residents when homes close down it raises very serious questions about whether privatised services can provide the stability and quality of care needed for vulnerable citizens.

Additional changes to the financing of public services include the use of new approaches such as social impact bonds. These are financial instruments which return a profit to investors in social care projects if these projects meet certain objectives in terms of measurable improvement in service users' circumstances. Bugg-Levine et al. (2012) suggest that greater 'precision and transparency' are needed in measuring social outcomes. This is a significant stumbling block to this type of funding. Measuring the outcomes of social work interventions is extremely difficult and it is something which the sector has never got to grips with. Do we conclude, for example, that a person with an alcohol problem has improved if they are sober six months after finishing a programme or do we have to wait until a year or two years after the intervention to decide if treatment has been successful? For services such as day care, finding a measure if improvement is even more elusive. Different service users will obtain different benefits and turning benefits into numerical measurements is extremely difficult. Each service user's situation is unique and each will have a different view about what represents improvement for them. There is also the issue of the supposed savings to the public purse, which allows the government to fund the return to investors in social impact bonds. A project which diverts service users from prison or psychiatric hospital will be of immense benefit to the service users who access it but will not necessarily generate cashable savings. As long as the prison or the psychiatric hospital remains open other people will be found to fill them or some beds will simply be left empty while the ward in which they sit still has to be staffed. Funding methods such as social impact bonds are interesting developments but I doubt if they will realise the high expectations which some people have for them. Most investors will put their money into the sector via funds which invest in a number of social projects to offset risk. For the sector as a whole to generate returns for investors the additional funding to successful projects will have to be greater than that lost by the unsuccessful ones. As the ultimate customer for social services is the government these additional returns will have to be financed through the public purse.

For field social workers, the prospect of the outsourcing of their jobs provides cause for concern but also opportunity. Jones (2015) warns of private companies, some of which have a poor reputation for public services, winning contracts to provide child protection services. An alternative possibility, however, is for social workers to form social work practices. By working at arm's length from the local authority social workers could take charge of their relationships with the communities they serve; practise in a way which more directly fits with their professional ethos; manage their public relations and public image better; reduce unnecessary bureaucracy; and equip their teams with better IT and be less risk averse in deploying it. It is in my opinion a certainty that social work services will be outsourced gradually throughout the country. If the danger of social work services going to unpopular companies is as significant as Professor Jones suggests then I believe it is imperative that social workers themselves take some control of the outsourcing process. They can do this by developing a model which safeguards working conditions and improves the quality of outcomes for service users. Unfortunately the high degree of negativity towards outsourcing from within the profession and social work academics seriously hampers the development of social-worker-led services. The predominant response is opposition to any change but without any political, media or public support it is difficult to see how the status quo can be maintained.

The Department for Education (2012) produced a report on an evaluation of a number of pilot children's social work practices. The report gave mixed findings but identified some benefits of social work practices as a model. A report on pilot adult social work practices by the Social Care Workforce Research Unit (2014) also reported mixed conclusions, not helped by the fact that the pilots looked at were varied in nature.

I would recommend that any social worker in fieldwork services reads this report and starts giving some thought to how they function within an outsourced service. It is important in my opinion that social workers are active agents in shaping changes to services and are not passive recipients in changes which are driven by others.

Shaping the future will be a real test of the resiliency of the profession and its ability to envision a positive future outside local authority control.

Chapter recap

In this chapter I reviewed some of the ways in which new technologies can improve the efficiency of social workers and some of the cultural obstacles to achieving the maximum benefits of technology. I looked at why some modern work practices such as agile working and hot desking have failed to be used effectively in social work and how they can be made to work by taking account of the professional needs of social workers as well as the pressure to reduce costs. The chapter also looked at changes in how services are funded and organised, and implications of this for the profession.

Further reading

There are various bloggers online talking about the use of technology in social work. If you want to read about innovations in the use of technology in the workplace the *Harvard Business Review* is an expensive but excellent source. It is available at larger news outlets in major cities or by subscription.

The *Financial Times* periodically runs articles on public sector finance issues. It is the most reliable source of information on these issues. *The Times* is another good source of reliable information on these issues. Both of these newspapers have pay-walls online. You can find out if they have salient articles by checking the front page of the print versions at your local newsstand if you are not a regular reader. The *Guardian* Social Care pages online are also an essential source of information about structural changes in social work as is the *Community Care* website. I would recommend subscribing to the email newsletter for both of these websites.

Next up!

In the next chapter I will look at how to develop good cooperative relationships in the workplace and how to deal with negative ones such as bullying and harassment.

6

FACING UP TO CONFLICT, DISCRIMINATION AND BULLYING IN THE WORKPLACE

Key Concepts and Issues in this Chapter

- Using active listening and reflective listening
- How stress affects communication
- Avoiding over-committing
- Bullying and social work
- Why bullies behave the way they do
- Bullies with serious psychological problems
- How to tackle bullying
- Organisational approaches to tackling bullying

Dealing with difficult people at work

In previous chapters we have considered the fact that social work involves a great deal of emotional labour and that this is a source of stress. In the next chapter we are going to look at the importance of supervision as a way of getting support with the emotional demands of the job. In this chapter, however, we look at how inter-personal issues with colleagues can be a source of stress in the workplace.

When I first started as a social worker I had very idealistic and naive views about what the temperament and attitudes of other social workers would be. I was shocked to be told by a colleague in another social work office that his manager regularly swore at him and bullied him. At different times in my career I have encountered some quite macho and authoritarian management cultures and also antagonism and conflict between colleagues. Despite the progressive aims of the profession, social workers are sometimes less than cordial in their relationships with each other. Interpersonal tension can be heightened by problems such as over-work, staff sickness, bureaucratic pressures, micro-management, and the ongoing backdrop of media hostility towards the profession. Sadly, even sexual and racist abuse can occur within social services organisations.

Before I go on to talk about bullying and how to counter it I would like to deal with the issue of how we communicate with people who are obstructive, argumentative, hostile or evasive. We can all find ourselves dealing with people in the workplace whom we would much rather avoid. These can be people who send us aggressive or annoying emails, or who are uncooperative when we ask them to do something straightforward and reasonable to help us.

Hasson (2015) suggests ways forward for dealing with difficult people. First of all she suggests active listening and showing that we are attentive. Of course, as social workers we are used to using these skills with service users. We may feel that it is unnecessary to state this and indeed some readers may feel insulted that I would even suggest that they need to practise active listening. It is after all what we do in our work. However, we can find ourselves working under a different set of assumptions when we are dealing with colleagues. We may feel that our opinion about something is self-evident. For example, let's say we are discussing how to go forward in a particular case. We may have examined all the information about the case and be very clear about what the correct decision is in terms of the law and the relevant codes of conduct and procedures. However, our manager or a colleague may have all the same information and have come to a very different conclusion. One of the modules which I have taught social worker students is Theories, Ethics and Values. It is a very interesting module because we explore how the way in which people reach decisions depends on the internal rules which they have for resolving ethical dilemmas. Some people will tend to have an approach we can term consequentialist. That is that they base their decision on the relative benefits of different possible outcomes. They believe that this is the way of best reaching a decision in individual cases. Other people tend to reach ethical judgements using a more rule-based approach. They do not see the decision in front of them in isolation but rather work from principles which can be applied equally to other decisions of a similar nature. They consider this to be a better way to make judgements because it reinforces rules which are fairer to people overall. Of course, people will not be divided neatly into two ways of reaching decisions. Most people will use combinations of these approaches to ethical decisions.

It is important to understand that someone may reach different decisions to us because they have used a different approach in making their judgement. This is why it is important to actively listen and try to understand why a colleague has reached their conclusion and demonstrate that we are doing this no matter how unreasonable their opinion might at first seem to us.

Hasson suggested that we adopt an approach to listening which she calls reflective listening. This is like the process which we might use in person-centred therapy when we reflect back to the client what they have said in order to improve our and their understanding. This involves repeating, summarising or paraphrasing what the other person has said. The purpose of this is to try to ensure that we have understood them properly and give them an opportunity to correct our interpretation. She acknowledged that a conversation would be very unnatural if this was done with everything the other person said but that if we listen as if we are going to do this then we are more likely to understand them properly. When we are discussing something with someone with whom we have a history of conflict we can sometimes go into the discussion with preconceptions of what they are going to say. As a consequence we can find ourselves filling in gaps between things which they say with our own assumptions about what they mean or their motivations. Reflective listening avoids this. It can also slow down the discussion and give both parties a chance to reflect on what they are saying rather than escalating any disagreement. This in turn can help both parties to remain calm and avoid resorting to shouting or becoming angry.

Another strategy which Hasson suggests is using open questions to help the other person to clarify their position. This is a way of showing we are genuinely interested in what they have to say and that we are not working on the basis of assumptions and preconceptions. Taking an interest in how someone actually feels about something is also important. It may be that something that we have said to them in the past or done has been interpreted as a criticism or a lack of regard for them. Actually asking someone how they feel about something gives them an opportunity to voice negative emotions and get issues and resentments out in the open.

Again, I apologise if you think I am coming across as patronising in suggesting these steps to you as a social worker. However, I know from my own experience that I do not always use the same standards of listening and communicating which I would have with service users when I am talking to colleagues.

Of course listening and empathising is only part of the equation in dealing with difficult people. We also have to be able to get across our own feelings and concerns to others and ideally in a way which is assertive rather than aggressive. This means taking ownership for our feelings and being able to express them in a clear, calm and coherent way. You need to be able to explain clearly what this issue is from your perspective, keep the discussion on track and on point. If we have done anything wrong then being willing to admit that is useful in defusing the situation.

Hasson advocates that if we are going to have to go into any kind of negotiation or bargaining with another person, then we should think carefully in advance about what outcome we are wanting to achieve, what things we are willing to compromise on and what things are non-negotiable. It is also important to be able to state what we want clearly. If we do this then we are less likely to find ourselves agreeing to something which we find unacceptable or reaching an impasse. If you are not used to being assertive with other people then this may be something which you need to practise. If assertiveness is something which you have always found difficult and you have doubts about your ability to change then you might want to consider doing an assertiveness training course or getting help from a therapist. Alternatively, there are a lot of good resources on the internet including videos on developing assertiveness.

Being aware of the effects of stress on communication

Field (2003) discussed the importance of being self-aware of our own communication style and how it can change when we are under stress. A particularly vulnerable area of communication which she identified is emails. This is a form of communication in which misunderstandings can occur at the best of times. However, when we are stressed we are even more likely than normal to send emails which can be curt or impolite. If we are feeling angry or stressed it may be better to delay sending emails or use an alternative form of communication such as the phone or going to speak to someone in person. Field stated that when the body is under stress the hormone cortisol shuts down the activity of neurones and it thus becomes more difficult to take in new information. This means that stressed people will be less able to take in new information or understand the subtleties of it. This can also be experienced as forgetfulness because new information is not retained. These effects of stress can increase the likelihood of miscommunication and misunderstanding. Field observed that stressed team members can be withdrawn. This increases the chance that they may fail to pass on important information to others or fail to successfully take in important information themselves. It is vital that team managers make contact with staff who withdraw themselves from contact with team members both from the point of view of inquiring about whether they need help and support but also to check that they do not have important dilemmas surrounding their cases which they have not shared. It is important to take heed of other people's communication styles with you and other people. If a colleague is communicating in a terse way with you and with other people then it could be a sign that they under stress. If, on the other hand, a number of people are showing signs of being hurt or annoyed with you then it may be that your communication to them is being affected by you being stressed.

Weeks (2001) set out three important rules for managing conversations when people are stressed or the subject matter is difficult or sensitive. First, communication should be honest and straightforward. If we have to give people bad news or tell them something they may not like then it is important not to avoid the important points by using euphemisms or not being completely honest. We can still be polite and courteous but at the same time be honest. Second, Weeks advocates use of a neutral tone which will avoid causing anxiety or escalating any tensions. Third, Weeks states that we should avoid using any threats or expressions of anger. Rather we should adopt what Weeks describes as 'temperate' phrasing.

Avoiding taking on too much

One type of conflict which many people shy away from is resisting requests to take on additional work even when they are already overcommitted. Some people will also regularly volunteer to take on additional work even when already over-stretched. One reason for this can be that they just do not realise how much work they have. I have already considered this problem in Chapter 4. If one does not have control of one's workload then it is difficult to make a judgement about whether one is actually at or near capacity workload. This is why it is important to track and manage one's work effectively. Other reasons for taking too much work can be either a lack of assertiveness or alternatively a lack of self-worth leading one to believe that our efforts are never quite good enough. Robinson (1997) suggests that using visualisation to imagine ourselves saying no to unfair demands is one way of preparing ourselves for dealing with situations in which we find it hard to be assertive. He also suggests that beginning to say no in real situations in which we are faced with unfair demands will help one to build up new patterns of response to these situations. Social work is a moral profession and one that puts the service of others at its heart. However, that does not mean that we should overburden ourselves with impossible workloads. It is important to balance the quantity of work we produce with quality. Taking on more work than one is able to reasonably achieve will inevitably result in mistakes and oversights.

Bullying at work

Bullying is something we normally associate with children and adolescents. Sadly, however, bullying is something which also occurs in adulthood and the workplace can be as cruel a place as any playground.

Van Heugten (2011) recognised that the issue of workplace bullying has been acknowledged and extensively researched in nursing but has largely gone undiscussed in social work. She referred to some earlier research which she had done (van Heugten, 2004) which investigated violence and bullying between workers. The types of bullying behaviours which her study identified included verbal putdowns, derogatory remarks, personal comments including remarks about appearance, insults, swearing, micro-management by superiors, excessive criticism, efforts to socially isolate the victim and interference with professional roles and tasks. Some participants in the study also reported rude behaviour and inattentiveness by managers during supervision or being denied information which was important to them performing their job effectively or being excluded from important decision making. Other behaviours reported included malicious gossip and the forming of alliances between some workers to the exclusion of others. Not all bullying occurs in the direction of superiors to their subordinates; one manager in the van Heugten study had been the subject of 'upward bullying' in which she was ganged up on by her staff. In her study, van Heugten found effects on victims including loss of self-confidence, loss of enjoyment from going to work, withdrawal from work projects, depression, anger towards the bully, hyper-vigilance and obsessive preoccupation with the bullying, depression and physical symptoms of stress.

Why do people bully?

Crawford (1992) stated that the origins of bullying behaviour can be traced back to early childhood when some children are disciplined very severely. He believed that the fear and resentment felt by the child can manifest itself in the adult as a determination not to be the vulnerable one again. Humiliating and dominating other people is a psychological defence mechanism to avoid being vulnerable oneself. By being aggressive towards other people they are trying to prevent anyone being able to hurt them. Crawford also suggested that narcissism as a result of having a very doting uncritical parent can lead some people to believe that they are perfect. This leads to hatred towards people who do not think they are wonderful and contempt for those who do. Sometimes jealousy about a colleague's success or apparent popularity can also be a motivation for bullying. Some bullies create an in-group of sycophants around them who are given special roles or selectively kept more informed about what is happening in the organisation. This type of arrangement enhances the power of the bully and makes it less likely that people will support the person/people being bullied as they risk being consigned to the out group.

Crawford suggested that some bullies will crumble quickly if challenged about their behaviour or reported. However, the ability to do this successfully is dependent on a workplace culture where people with genuine complaints are supported.

Bullies with serious psychological problems

Lubit (2004) listed a number of categories of what he called 'toxic managers': narcissistic managers, unethical managers, aggressive managers, rigid managers and impaired managers. Narcissistic managers are people with poor capacity for empathy and self-esteem which is simultaneously over-inflated and fragile. They defend against their low self-esteem by demeaning others. Sometimes, narcissism can be manifested in a need to control and micro-manage other people and sometimes in extreme paranoia and an irrational fear of being contradicted or undermined.

Unethical managers is a category which Lubit used for managers who indulge in unethical or exploitative behaviour such as sexually inappropriate behaviour or stealing from their employer. The category of aggressive managers includes bullies and managers who are ruthless and unfeeling. Some aggressive managers will happily scapegoat other staff to avoid criticism of themselves. Also within this category Lubit includes volatile managers who are liable to explode in angry outbursts. Lubit stated that emotional volatility can be a result of depression, burnout or anxiety. Rigid managers are people who can be dogmatic, authoritarian, obsessive and prone to micro-managing others. They are perfectionists and cannot trust others to do their job in their own way, but rather believe that there is only one right way to do things. Impaired managers are those suffering from serious untreated psychological problems, psychiatric illness or substance misuse problems. In common with the other categories, they can be unpredictable and difficult to deal with in addition to failing to consistently give the support and guidance which their subordinates will expect from them.

Having an understanding of the problems which may underlie a bullying boss's (or colleague's) behaviour may help us to decide how best to cope with their behaviour. If we are victims of unfair treatment by a manager or a colleague who we cannot easily avoid then this can be very distressing and adversely affect our enjoyment of work.

Dealing with bullying

When the bully is your manager, the best strategy may be to look for another job. This is not always easy to do. First of all you have to recognise that you are being bullied. The fact that bullies undermine self-confidence has two important consequences. First, the victim may begin to believe that they are as useless and incompetent as the bully is trying to make them feel. This can, bizarrely, involve liking the bully and wanting to gain their approval. Winter (2015) coined the term Stockholm bias (based on the term Stockholm Syndrome) to describe a situation in which the victim is disproportionately grateful for any show of approval by the bullying manager. Remember, part of the strategy of the bully is to undermine the self-esteem of the victim so that they become dependent on the bully as a source of validation. Another problem with being a victim of bullying is that if one is feeling despondent and low in self-confidence it is going to be more difficult to sell oneself in the competitive job market.

It is important not to start a new job which is inappropriate just to leave an unhappy situation. This could undermine your confidence even more. It is helpful in these situations to begin the process of thinking about what you are going to do next. In Chapter 9 I will be talking about the benefits of putting together an up-to-date CV as a way of clarifying your views and intentions in relation to work. For someone who is facing unfair treatment and oppression in the workplace, the act of putting together a CV and reflecting on their skills can provide important reminders of how experienced and skilled they really are. It can form part of a healing process towards the restoration of self-confidence.

Lubit (2004) described the value of emotional intelligence in dealing with a situation in which we are bullied. He advocates that emotional intelligence can help us to identify problematic or dangerous situations at an early stage and also to deal with them as tactically and skilfully as possible if they arise. Lubit stated that if we can understand that someone else's bad behaviour is due to stress of psychological problems in them, then it can help us to take their bad behaviour less personally. Emotional intelligence can also prevent us from going into a flight or fight response in which we can resort to behaviours which escalate conflict or which are damaging to us. Lubit stated that personal beliefs, such as thinking it is weak to back down in the face of aggression, can get in the way of us dealing with conflict in a way which is going to be most beneficial to us. Lubit stated that it is actually a stronger response to show the ability to walk away from a pointless conflict. He also suggested that therapy or coaching can be useful in helping to clarify for us what has happened and how to move on from it.

Organisational responses to bullying

Many organisations take pride in displaying kitemarks such as Investors in People or displaying credentials such as 'Respect at work' policies. However, these displays of being a caring employer are not always translated into reality for all the workers who are employed there. Van Heugten (2011) stated that conduct policies are not in themselves enough to prevent or tackle bullying. She stated that these policies need to be actively implemented. One way of doing this is training all staff to identify and intervene in behaviour which is discriminatory or humiliating. By 'listening' to their own emotional reactions and intervening by interrupting or deflecting bullying behaviour staff can all take a role in tackling bullying. Staff can also take a role by positively behaving in ways which are inclusive if they see colleagues being marginalised or ignored. Everybody can take a role in performing and modelling inclusive behaviour. This is especially important where there are elements of sexism or racism in the bullying behaviour. Everyone can play a part in changing the culture of their organisation by challenging bullying or excluding behaviour and by demonstrating inclusive and supportive behaviour. Van Heugten identified restructuring and other forms of organisational change as flashpoints for bullying. This may be because of the additional stress caused by change and resulting increases in workloads or because of confusion about new roles and responsibilities.

Victims of bullying can get support and advice from their trade union. I can't emphasise enough how important it is to join a union and ideally this should be the principal one which is recognised by your employer for people of your profession. The right time to join is the week you start your employment. If you try to join when you need help then you may find that the union will not represent you for a period of several months. This is to prevent people from opportunistically joining when they need support and then resigning when they no longer need help. Being a member of a union involves taking collective responsibility for the welfare of your colleagues.

You can help colleagues who are bullied or sexually harassed by being willing to be a witness for them if you have seen these types of behaviour. It is also important to stand up and be counted by opposing bullying if you see it happening and by not colluding with discriminatory or excluding behaviour. Bullying, discrimination and harassment are everybody's business.

Chapter recap

In this chapter we looked at the difficulties in dealing with difficult people in a work setting. We looked at how emotionally intelligent communication can be used to improve relationships with difficult people. We looked at the issue of bullying in social services organisations, the reasons why people bully and how everyone has a role in tackling bullying and discrimination in their workplace.

There were no exercises in this chapter. Although this is the approach used elsewhere in the book, I didn't feel it was appropriate for this chapter. There are techniques described in this chapter which you may well wish to try if you are experiencing these problems. However, I think that any strategy which you use in dealing with bullies should be chosen carefully after a lot of thought and, if possible, discussion with people whom you trust.

Further reading

If you have serious problems with a manager I would recommend reading *Coping with Toxic Managers, Subordinates and Other Difficult People* by Roy Lubit. For a good overview of stress in social work settings I would recommend *Social Work Under Pressure* by Kate van Heugten. A trade union representative will be able to inform you of your rights and opportunities for redress if you are a victim of unfair practices at work.

Next up!

In the next chapter I will look in depth at social work supervision. The term 'reflective supervision' is used regularly in social work literature but what does genuinely reflective supervision consist of? I will look at the value of supervision contracts and supervision records in improving the quality of supervision. I will also consider the value of different approaches to supervision such as group supervision and action learning sets. The chapter will finish with a look at the value of building and maintaining good professional networks as part of your career development.

7

MAKING THE MOST OF SUPERVISION AND OTHER SOURCES OF SUPPORT

Key Concepts and Issues in this Chapter

- The importance of supervision
- Functions of supervision
- Defining and understanding reflective supervision
- Enhancing reflective supervision through mindfulness
- The 10 key elements of mindful reflective supervision
- Becoming a supervisor
- Forming a supervision contract
- Preparing for and recording supervision
- Putting into practice the learning from supervision
- Reviewing and evaluating supervision
- Alternative approaches – group supervision and action learning
- Building a supportive network

Good supervision is absolutely fundamental to good social work. It is a highly complex job with serious ramifications if mistakes are made. It is also, as we have discussed in earlier chapters, a job with a great deal of emotional labour. And yet many social workers are not receiving the support and guidance which they require. In 2013 the *Community Care* website (McGregor, 2013) published the results of a piece of research involving 601 practitioners, student social workers and managers which found that one-third of participants claimed not to be receiving any supervision and of those who received it over half claimed that their supervision was not reflective. These findings went against the recommendations of the Social Work Reform Board which had stated over two years previously that social workers should receive reflective supervision at least monthly and ideally by a registered social worker. Of the reasons given for supervision not being provided the most common reasons were manager turnover or that supervision was not prioritised in the agency. In quotes from respondents some reported being bullied or threatened by managers and a large percentage felt that supervision was too focused on performance targets and timescales. As a result, many of those who did receive regular supervision found it a negative experience.

Another problem emerged for social workers who were part of multi-disciplinary teams and were line managed by professionals from other disciplines. In these situations there was lack of clarity about exactly who was responsible for different elements of social work supervision.

It is possible, of course, that there was a degree of self-selection in the *Community Care* survey and that perhaps people who felt strongly about the issue (as a result of negative experiences) were more likely to respond. However, the results do point to an unsatisfactory experience of supervision for some workers.

Manthorpe et al. (2015) reported considerable variation in social workers' experiences of supervision. They stated that there was a tapering effect with more experienced social workers receiving less support than newly qualified social workers. Time constraints were given as the reason by managers for social workers not always receiving an ideal amount of supervision.

Exercise

What Represents Good Supervision for You?

Before we go on to a discussion of the purpose of supervision I would like you to reflect on what you think are the important functions of supervision for you. List them in order and for each one list what you feel your supervisor is doing to ensure these needs are provided for, what you are doing to help your supervisor support you in these areas and in the last column listing how this element of supervision could be improved.

I have filled out an example of what a row could look like.

Table 8

Functions of supervision in order of importance to me	How these functions are provided by my supervisor	How I help my supervisor to provide these elements in supervision	How these functions of supervision could be improved
For example	For example	For example	For example
1. Emotional support	1. By being willing to listen patiently when I talk about my feelings	1. By reflecting on what things I have found difficult to cope with before coming to supervision so that I can come prepared to talk about them	1. By my supervisor ensuring that we always have a quiet room and the supervision time is free from interruptions

Reflecting on your responses were there any surprises about either the order you listed the different purposes of supervision or the degree to which they are supported by you and your supervisor? If there are any insights in your last column about how your supervision could be improved then you may want to constructively take these insights into your next supervision.

Key functions of supervision

Before going on to look at how supervision can be improved I will first set out the traditional model of social work supervision. Kadushin and Harkness (2002) described three components of good supervision:

1. Administrative/managerial – maintenance of standards.
2. Educative/formative – developing skills and abilities.
3. Supportive /restorative – enabling reflection.

Wilson et al. (2008) described this traditional approach as casework supervision where the focus was on talking through the details of specific cases which social workers were engaged with and offering support and guidance where necessary. They indicate that this has been replaced for many workers with what they call case management supervision. This approach has much less emphasis on development of workers and more emphasis on managing how the worker meets managerial targets.

Noble and Irwin (2009) stated that as a result of financial cutbacks and a more conservative political climate, social work supervision had become more focused on efficiency, accountability and performance and less on developing the worker professionally or dealing with problems in their cases. They also reported that lack of opportunity for reflection was having a negative effect on social workers' morale.

Looking back at the exercise which you did earlier in the chapter, was reflection an important part of supervision for you? I am fairly certain that it will have been and that you will probably have used reflective practice or a similar term. The importance of reflective practice is emphasised throughout social work education programmes and supervision is a logical forum for facilitating it. The Professional Capabilities Framework (BASW, 2012c) is designed to encourage development throughout a social worker's career. Social workers have a commitment to developing professionally throughout their career and to constantly trying to improve the quality of their practice while ensuring that it is ethically sound. Just as any top athlete needs an excellent coach, the standards which professional social workers aspire to require the encouragement and supervision of a skilled and experienced supervisor. When supervision becomes an exercise in administrative routine this is a source of frustration and disappointment. The confidential nature of social work and the emotional material which social workers deal with also means that only someone bound by confidentiality and with the necessary professional understanding can help the social worker with the emotional labour inherent in the job role.

McGregor (2013) referred to the analysis of the evidence about the importance of good supervision which had been carried out by Professor John Carpenter. He found that there was a lack of good published research about the impact of good supervision and it was not often clear in the research exactly what the nature of the supervision in the studies was. However, good supervision was found to be correlated with job satisfaction, worker retention, employee perception of support from their employer and employer perceptions of worker effectiveness. Correlation does not of course prove that good supervision is what causes these benefits but it seems at least that good quality supervision and a positive working environment go hand in hand.

A definition of reflective supervision

It is worth pausing for a moment to think about what we actually mean by reflective practice and how reflective supervision might make this easier. Knott and Scragg (2010) trace the idea to John Dewey (1933, 1938). They stated that Dewey believed that reflection was 'the continual re-evaluation of personal beliefs, assumptions and ideas in the light of experience and data and the generation of alternative interpretations of those experiences and data' (p.5). Knott and Scragg stated that some writers are of the view that reflective practice is a different approach from evidence-based practice or at least that they are at opposite ends of a continuum. This is an odd conclusion as Dewey's explanation of reflection is very similar to the scientific method in which hypotheses are tested and then refined in the light of further findings. Evidence-based practice need not be a 'top down process' as Healy (2005) seems to suggest it is. When we visit a General Practitioner or physician their diagnosis and intervention will be heavily evidence based. However, their relationship and prior knowledge of the patient will influence how they go about their diagnosis and their treatment plan should take into account the concerns and views of their patient. Thus, even the most scientifically driven parts of health and social care depend on communication, understanding and empathy. In turn, decisions made by physicians in the treatment of large numbers of individual patients will influence health policy. In social work, of course, empathic communication with the service user is much more central to the caring relationship and social workers usually deal with much more complex situations and problems. The infinite diversity and uniqueness of social work cases make the application of evidence and the measuring of outcomes much more difficult than they are within medicine. That does not mean that we should not attempt to discover and learn from evidence.

Knott and Scragg (2010) described two reflective processes explored in the work of Donald Schön (2002): reflection-on-action and reflection-in-action. The former process involves thinking about what was done, what theories or techniques were used, what knowledge or understanding has been gained and what can be learned for the future. It is this process which is facilitated by reflective supervision. By providing the practitioner a safe space within a relationship of trust the supervisor can use questions, challenges, observations and constructive feedback to facilitate reflection. Schön's other reflective approach, the process of reflection-in-action, involves carefully thinking about our practice while we are doing it. This could be renamed mindful practice. Obviously this practice takes place outside supervision. However, good supervision, especially when it has an element of coaching, can promote a mindful and reflective approach within the worker. The worker can internalise elements of the supervisor and incorporate elements of their style within their own internal dialogue.

Some writers, notably Fook (2002) and Banks (2012), promote the concept of reflexive practice, often in a way which suggests that it is superior to reflective practice. I have not seen the term defined in a way which makes it distinguishable or measurably different from good reflective practice. Like a number of concepts in contemporary social work theory it is more of an article of faith than something which can actually be demonstrated. I will avoid further discussion of the concept as I think it actually makes exploration of reflective practice and reflective supervision more difficult.

The requirement for reflective supervision

The Local Government Association Standards for Employers of Social Workers in England (LGA, 2014a) state that social workers should be provided with 'high quality, regular supervision'. While the standard does not specifically use the term 'reflective supervision' it does say 'Supervision should challenge students and qualified practitioners to reflect critically on their practice and should foster an inquisitive approach to social work' (Standard 5). Thus the standard is setting out an approach to supervision which requires challenge and reflection in addition to encouraging the student to engage with research and seek to constantly improve their practice. The standard also requires supervision to be regular and of at least 1.5 hours' uninterrupted time. Employers who do not provide this quality of supervision for their staff on a regular basis are in breach of the standards agreed for all employers of registered social workers that regulatory bodies such as CQC and Ofsted will expect employers to abide by. Where social workers are dissatisfied with the quality of supervision which they are getting they can point to the guidelines and trade unions should be supportive in helping social workers to deal with concerns of this nature. It is worth pointing out that in the event of any inquiry into poor practice, an employer who did not follow these guidelines would be open to criticism.

The other source of support for reflective practice and by extension reflective supervision is the Professional Capabilities Framework for Social Work (BASW, 2012c). One of the professional capabilities is 'critical reflection'. At the level of qualified social worker the worker is expected to 'routinely and efficiently apply critical reflection and analysis to increasingly complex cases'.

Knowledge and Skills statements have now been published (Department for Education, 2015). This includes direction on the responsibilities of supervisors to provide 'emotionally intelligent practice supervision' and 'promote reflective thinking'. There are also suggestions in the statements about the use of 'peer supervisor' and 'group case consultation' to help identify 'identity bias' and 'shift thinking'.

Key elements of mindful reflective supervision

Wonnacott (2012) advocated an integrated approach to supervision in which there is attention to all the different functions of supervision.

I would like to take this concept a stage further and argue that supervision should be reflective, integrated *and* mindful. Within the context of social work Lynn (2010: 290) described mindfulness as 'moment to moment awareness or paying attention to the moment without judgement'. A non-judgemental attitude is of course an important attribute of social work practice. Within the context of social work supervision it allows the social worker space to recognise and admit to mistakes as well as recognise successes and grow as a result of these insights. The heightened awareness by both parties helps to ensure that important information and insights are captured and processed.

The reflection should take place on the part of both the supervisee and supervisor. Both the supervisor and supervisee should take responsibility for trying to maintain an integrative approach in which they keep in touch with the different purposes of supervision. Thus while the supervisee's main focus may be on getting direction and support in their casework they also maintain an awareness of their developmental needs and bigger picture issues such as ideas for how their service could be improved. Similarly, the supervisor must not let their need for managing workload and performance get in the way of providing support for the worker and promoting their development. The reflective supervision becomes mindful when there is an awareness of and an acceptance of feelings which we have about our work and a relationship of trust in which these can be shared and their meanings be better understood.

I would like to expand on Kadushin's list of the purposes of supervision which I introduced earlier. I propose that good social work supervision must contain the following 10 elements and that they must be part of an integrated approach.

10 key elements of mindful reflective supervision

1. Space for and facilitation of reflection and self-evaluation of practice

The LGA guidelines recommend 1.5 hours of uninterrupted time. This can be difficult for busy managers who frequently have to respond to urgent queries. However, these problems can be mitigated by not over-scheduling on days when supervision is being carried out so that if there are interruptions or delays in starting, the time can be made up. The knowledge and skills statements for practice supervisors advocate 'emotionally intelligent' supervision to 'promote reflective practice'. Social workers also have a responsibility for being fully present and focused in their supervision meetings and not letting their mind drift to all the tasks they have to complete after the supervision is over.

2. Guidance and direction on cases

This is the traditional task which we associate with supervision. The supervisor is normally someone with more experience in the field than those they are supervising and supervision is a formal opportunity to pass on that knowledge and experience. Where the social worker is being managed by someone who is not social work qualified it is important that the clinical or professional element of supervision is provided by another person who is a social worker.

Statement 2 of the Statements for Practice Supervisors (DfE, 2015) states that supervisors and Should 'facilitate the use of best evidence to devise effective interventions'. The statement also states that supervisors should also recognise where there is a need for them to be educative and when they should help the practitioner to draw on their own knowledge and experience. To do this effectively, supervisors need to have an understanding and awareness of the experience of the staff and in turn supervisees have to be open about their experience, expertise and where they recognise that they have learning needs.

3. Managing caseload and other elements of workload

This is the managerial part of supervision. Ideally this should be provided by the same person as at point 2 above, as they will be aware of the pressures which the worker is under. It is possible to have what appears to be a manageable caseload on paper yet be under a great deal of pressure and stress if one's cases are especially complex or several service users are in a state of crisis. It is important therefore that even where these supervisory roles are split there is an acknowledgement that case allocation cannot be done in a purely mechanical way. Using a workloading system is one way to try to make caseload management fairer and easier. However, as has been noted elsewhere, the unpredictable and diverse nature of social work tasks makes it difficult for workloading systems to capture the demands of a caseload accurately.

4. Performance management and feedback

Statement 2 of the knowledge and skills Statements for Practice Supervisors makes reference to the need to 'Develop a culture of learning and improvement, where staff are sufficiently stretched and mentored to meet their aspirations'. An important part of supervision is giving staff feedback on their performance, giving praise where appropriate, and giving help and guidance to improve performance.

5. Coaching

Statement 8 of the knowledge and skills Statements for Practice Supervisors makes reference to a need for a 'commitment to continued improvement'. An important way to do this is to adopt a coaching approach to encouraging staff. If this is provided by the manager or supervisor then it is likely to be more of an attitudinal approach within the supervisory relationship – that of a mixture of encouragement and constructive challenge. However, anyone who wants to radically tackle some aspect of their performance such as report writing, time management or some aspect of engagement with service users could consider entering a formal coaching relationship with someone outside of their department. Many local authorities have members of staff who have been trained in performance coaching. Irrespective of where the coaching dynamic takes place it is important that social workers get encouragement and challenge to keep them positively engaged with their job and doing the best job they can for service users.

6. Emotional support

We have already noted that social work is a job with a great deal of emotional labour. Supervision can be an important source of that support. In a good supervisory relationship where there is a great deal of trust then this can be provided here. However, where there is a less well-developed relationship or where a worker needs to discuss deeper emotional issues which have been brought up by a particular piece of work they may wish to consider non-managerial supervision. I received non-managerial supervision from a psychodynamic therapist in the early days of my career. I had to pay for it but it was money well spent and gave me a lot of insight into how I felt emotionally about my work. I had some reservations about some aspects of the statutory social work task and I felt these were bigger picture issues which I could not cover in my supervision with my manager as they were not directly related to casework.

7. Managing personal developmental needs

Financial resources for staff development opportunities can be restricted in an environment of austerity. However, all staff should have their development needs considered on an ongoing basis. Not all developmental needs require attendance at expensive courses. Sometimes reference to a policy document or attending a meeting as an observer will suffice for some needs. In the integrated approach advocated by Wonnacott, developmental needs should be identified as part of the normal discussion of supervision. This aspect of supervision should not be left for annual appraisals.

8. Taking feedback for improving efficiency and effectiveness and quality of the service

Supervision offers managers an opportunity to receive information and insights which will help them to improve the service. In the next chapter we will look more closely at Lean approaches to improving social work services. If a manager has a Lean orientation and is supervising mindfully they will have an ability to identify through the accounts of their workers, where agency procedures could be made more efficient. They should listen and respond enthusiastically and constructively to the insights and suggestions of their workers. Service improvement is everyone's business and it is important for workers to know that managers take complaints about bureaucracy seriously.

9. Supervision which is emotionally aware

This means being aware of the interpersonal dynamics both of the supervisory relationship and also of the relationships between the social worker and his/her service users and other colleagues and how these different relationships influence practice and the supervisory process. Statement 7 of the knowledge and skills Statements for Practice Supervisors makes reference to 'emotionally intelligent practice supervision'.

Wonnacott (2012: 89) described an emotionally intelligent supervisor as one who is 'attuned to the emotional impact of social work practice and able to recognise and manage her own emotional responses so as to be able to recognise and respond to the emotional content of discussions with supervisees'.

Wonacott (2012) explained the importance of understanding the phenomena of transference and having an awareness of these when they occur in supervision. An emotionally aware, mindful approach to supervision will help to ensure that these phenomena are identified and overcome. Wonnacott gives an example of 'mirroring' in which a social worker forgot in supervision to discuss a foster carer who made it difficult for her to see foster children on their own. Wonnacott stated that this led to the foster children's voices being absent in supervision just as they were in the social worker's practice. Understood in psychodynamic terms, aspects of the real-world relationships are being played out in supervision.

Wonnacott (2012) suggests that for a good supervision relationship to be established the supervisor has to properly establish all three sources of his/her authority:

1. Role authority – this comes from the power given to the job role by the employer but it is still important to establish this in the relationship itself. For people who have been internally promoted it can be important to establish themselves in the new supervisory role with colleagues who had previously been their peers. Alternatively, it may be that the previous person who occupied the role did not use their authority appropriately or authoritatively. In that situation it may be necessary to educate supervisees about how the role is properly understood within the culture of the organisation.
2. Professional authority – deriving from the supervisor's knowledge and experience. This is something which can be established by the supervisor bringing their knowledge to the supervision without undermining the supervisee's confidence or inhibiting their potential for directing their own growth.
3. Personal authority – based on who the supervisor is and how they manage and present themselves. This build-up of personal confidence and trust is something which needs to be earned by the supervisor and built upon gradually through a relationship which is attentive and caring.

10. Promoting mindful reflective practice

By demonstrating supervision which is emotionally aware the supervisor can encourage a mindful approach to practice by the social worker in which they are attuned to service users' feelings and their own emotions while in practice.

When emotional awareness, authoritativeness, encouragement, support and challenge are combined in a conscious, mindful way we can say that we have an approach to supervision which is genuinely holistic and nurturing.

Becoming a supervisor

In the last section we explored the components of good supervision and looked at the need to establish different sources of authority in the supervisory relationship. Kadushin and Harkness (2002) stated that going from practitioner to supervisor was analogous to a major life transition in which there is a period of disruption and depression followed by personal growth. It involves disengaging from one role and taking on a new one. They argued that while being a practitioner has an emphasis on expressive behaviours (such as showing empathy and compassion), supervision involves a greater emphasis on instrumental behaviours (such as organising and co-ordinating).

I would argue that while there is a change in emphasis, good supervision must include these caring elements with the proviso that the therapeutic element of the relationship cannot be unconditional to the degree that it can in relationships with the service user. The supervisor/manager has to sometimes exercise authority where there is a difference of opinion about the appropriate course of action in casework.

Kadushin and Harkness also argue that there is a shift from process to product. The supervisor has to be much more aware of the wider responsibilities and objectives of the agency. Additional changes may be a feeling that one has to be more responsible and be a role model for staff, setting the tone for the team. There is also the problem if simultaneously having to manage stress and pressures of workers and manage the expectations and demands of the agency.

Kadushin and Harkness also explored some of the issues which occur where there are race or gender differences between supervisor and supervisee. They point out that if a white supervisor ignores the race of a black supervisee, then this can be experienced by the supervisee as a negation of their black identity. Issues can also arise in relation to workers encountering racism within the field. The supervisor should give the worker space to discuss these issues without treating them in a way which demeans their personal strengths and ability to cope. Kadushin and Harkness suggest an approach which shows sensitivity to race while being relaxed about it. Black supervisors can also have additional pressures. Vargus (1980) stated that ethnic minority managers can face pressure to act as advocates or representatives of the ethnic group from which they come.

Social work is a predominantly female profession though males are more predominant in management roles. Dailey (1983) found that male negativity towards being supervised by a woman was much less likely in social work than in the wider workforce. However, Petty and Odewahn (1983) found that men can react negatively to assertive behaviours by female supervisors.

If we are carrying out supervision mindfully we should have an awareness of how dynamics of personal characteristics of supervisor and supervisee affect our work together.

Forming a supervision contract

Creating a contract can be a useful process for the establishment of a successful supervision relationship. The contract sets out what the responsibilities are of each party in the supervision.

This can be especially useful where the managerial and professional elements of supervision are split between supervisors. In these situations the contract(s) can help to define where responsibility for the different elements of supervision should sit.

Hawkins and Shohet (2006) in their book *Supervision in the Helping Professions* recommend that a supervision contract should cover the following six areas:

1. Practicalities including arrangements for meeting, length and frequency of sessions, how privacy and possible interruptions will be dealt with.
2. Boundaries – clarifying confidentiality issues and how personal material which emerges in supervision will be dealt with.
3. Working alliance – exploration of what style of supervision is going to be helpful for the supervisee in light of their learning style and the supervision style of the supervisor.
4. Session format – how the supervision sessions will be structured including what sort of preparation the supervisee is expected to do in advance of the session and how an agenda will be set for sessions.
5. Organisational context – expectations of the agency which are likely to impact on supervision, including appraisal processes and how supervision feeds into them and any departmental policies or procedures surrounding supervision.
6. Note taking – what format supervision records will take and who is responsible for writing them.

A contract can help to manage expectations on both sides. In an earlier section of this chapter I set out a list of 10 components which I feel are essential to good mindful reflective supervision. I would suggest adding to the Hawkins and Shohet list an additional section which clarifies how supervision is going to address the elements of reflective supervision and how each will achieved in the supervision relationship. There is a danger of going into a supervisory relationship where the supervisor views the main purpose of supervision as performance management around targets whereas the supervisee expects a focus on emotional support. Clarifying these issues should help ensure that the needs of both parties are met through an explicit recognition of the different functions which the supervisory relationship is aiming to achieve. Of course it will not be possible at all times to cover all of the aspects of mindful supervision but making a commitment to them or clarifying which elements must be met within another forum or supervisory relationship will ensure that workers get the support they need.

Exercise

Reviewing Your Supervision Contract

If you are in a job with an existing supervisory relationship then review your existing supervision contract. Does it meet the requirements of the model we have discussed in this chapter? Does it meet all the aspects of mindful reflective supervision? If it does not meet all these aspects does it specify where else these needs will be met?

If you do not have a supervision contract then consider whether it might be helpful for you and your supervisor to draw one up as part of a review of supervision. If you have a desire to improve the quality or scope of your supervision then this exercise could be an opportunity to enter into a dialogue to achieve this.

Preparing for supervision sessions

I have already considered how important supervision time is and how a supervision contract can help ensure it delivers to the expectations of both parties.

However, to gain the most from each individual supervision session it is important to come prepared with an agenda of what you want to cover.

One way of doing this is to come with a list of cases which you need to discuss in order of priority. By doing this you can prioritise cases which are complex or which you require urgent guidance on. You may of course want to deal with some routine queries in supervision first. However, by flagging up to your supervisor that you have complex cases to be discussed you can ensure that time is reserved for them. An alternative or additional way of planning an agenda for supervision is to group issues thematically. For example: complex case discussion; routine queries about cases; cases for closure; clarification on procedural issues; intra- and inter-agency issues; personal issues; developmental needs. If you find a structure like this helpful then you may want to structure all your regular supervision sessions in the same way, allowing for variation where necessary. It is helpful to consider which cases or issues might fall under each heading in good time before the session commences. If you can come up with an agenda at least a day before the supervision session then this can be sent to your supervisor to help them prepare for the session. If you have queries about departmental procedures or policies, for example, then listing these for your supervisor before the session will give them time to gather up any documents that might be relevant to your discussion. If you want to discuss, for example, a draft report you are writing, then if you send the report to your supervisor before the session they may able to read it in advance rather than them having to use valuable supervision time to read it.

Exercise

Preparation for Supervision

If you do not normally prepare an agenda for supervision then try doing so as an experiment. Think of the different categories which you might want to use to structure your discussion. If possible send the agenda in advance to your supervisor.

Here is a possible structure to use.

Table 9

	Category	Examples
1.	Complex cases	e.g. Case 1, problems with foster placement
		Case 2, due report of type which I have not written before
		Case 3, difficulty in engaging with new service user
2.	Routine case issues	Case closures, resources needed for ongoing cases, etc.
3.	Procedural issues	Checking on referral procedure for local service
4.	Organisational issues	e.g. Concerns about lack of available desk space at hot desking facilities
		e.g. Observations about how risk assessment form could be improved
5.	Personal issues	Ongoing family health issues and flexible working arrangements
6.	Performance feedback	Review of progress made on developmental issues identified at last appraisal
7.	Developmental issues	Conference on diversity issues and adoption which I would like to attend

Record of supervision

Having a good clear and fair record of supervision is essential to making the most of the opportunities which supervision has for personal development and improving practice. Any action plans which are agreed in relation to improving performance such as better time management need to be recorded so that the worker has an understanding of what is expected of them. Discussion of personal issues should not be recorded in detail. However, a record can be made in very general terms of the fact that support was offered for personal issues if that is acceptable to the worker.

Wonnacott (2012) draws a very important distinction between which aspects of discussion of cases should be recorded in the supervision records and which should be recorded in the case file of individual supervision records. Service user names should not be mentioned in the supervision record and any decision which is reached about a particular service user should be recorded in the case records of the service user. In the case record you should include the date of the discussion and record the fact that the decision was reached as a result of a discussion in supervision.

Taking the lessons from supervision forward

To get the most from supervision we must have a mechanism for growing and developing through putting into practice the insights which we achieve through supervision. Morrison (2005) proposes that supervision works developmentally through a cyclical process of learning. The supervisee reports their experiences of doing their casework. The supervisor will ask questions to tease out more detail. The supervisor will promote the worker's reflection on their experiences by using prompts, paraphrasing and questions which encourage deeper thinking about what has happened and how it fits with previous experiences and social work theories. These discussions will help the supervisor and supervisee to arrive at conclusions about the meaning of what has happened. From this the supervisor and supervisee can agree on an action plan which the worker will then put into practice. The experiences and outcomes of the actions or interventions will then feed into the next supervision session, causing the cycle to be repeated.

If the worker adopts a mindful approach to their work then the processes of reflection and analysis will continue outside of supervision sessions. The worker should be conscious of the impact of their interactions with the service user in real time. They should adapt their approach according to the responses of the service user and the issues and material which the service user brings. Sometimes the prompts and suggestions made by the supervisee will continue to stimulate reflection long after the session in which they were made. When I had non-managerial supervision as a new worker years ago I did not always realise the full significance of prompts and challenges from the supervisor during the sessions. It was only later when I got back into work situations that I gained more profound insights into my practice and my attitudes to it. A good supervisor can have a presence in our mind even when we are not in supervision. We can imagine the sorts of challenges they might make of us and thereby practise more critically and more mindfully.

It is important that learning from supervision is seen as a two-way street. Item 8 in the list of components of mindful reflective supervision given earlier was 'taking feedback for improving efficiency and effectiveness and quality of the service'. It is important that suggestions from staff about service improvement are taken seriously. There is nothing more frustrating for workers than repeatedly raising issues about aspects of their workplace which get in the way of doing a good job without any acknowledgment or meaningful consideration of their suggestions. Where there are good reasons why a procedure which appears to be bureaucratic has to be carried out in the existing way then this should be explained to the supervisee in a manner which values their enthusiasm for improving the service. Where a good or viable suggestion is made then the supervisor should make it clear what they intend to do next with the suggestion. In some cases this may simply be to implement the suggestion forthwith. In other cases it could be to pass the suggestion up to a senior manager or to open the issue up for discussion at a team meeting to see if there is a consensus.

Managers who adopt a Lean approach should always be open to suggestions from staff for service improvement.

Evaluation of supervision

Having established a supervision contract and a structure or format for supervision it is useful to agree a point at which this will be evaluated. This review point can be a good opportunity to discuss whether supervision is meeting the expectations and needs of the supervisor and supervisee. At this point the contract and the regular supervision agenda can be amended if necessary.

Group supervision

Another approach to supervision is group supervision. There can be advantages to this approach in that participants can hear about other workers' experiences. This can be reassuring in that less confident colleagues can hear that other people can make mistakes just like them. However, there is equally a risk that there can be competitiveness with some participants being keen to trumpet their own successes. The person facilitating the supervision needs to be aware of group dynamics and should ideally have experience of working with groups in addition to being experienced in supervision. The group leader simultaneously needs to be aware of the content of what is being shared and its meaning while attending to the interactions and emotions of group members. This is a very difficult and demanding role. Spending time at the beginning of the supervisory relationship in setting out expectations, group rules, etc. is just as important in group supervision as in a one-to-one supervisory relationship.

Action learning sets

Action learning is an approach which has some similarities to group supervision. I feel that it is more appropriate for helping people to develop strategies to practical problems in their work than fulfilling the normal functions of supervision. Normally a stable group of between five and seven participants meet regularly for a defined number of meetings. There are a number of techniques which can be applied to dealing with the problems raised. My experience of being part of a set was that each member was given a slot to raise an issue or problem in their work. The person with the issue would leave the room while the rest of the group discussed the problem. They were then brought in to receive feedback and suggestions. Each person then feeds back to the next meeting about what progress they have made in dealing with the concerns which they discussed. This feedback element helps maintain the focus on action.

While action learning is a practical technique borrowed from the business world, developmental work has been carried out by Skills for Care in adapting the technique for social work by prioritising critical reflection within the process. They published a study (Skills for Care, 2014) evaluating the impact of a variation on action learning, which they termed 'critically reflective action learning'. The report gave a cautious endorsement to the process though I remain of the belief that action learning is more suitable as a practical intervention for clearly defined problems than a forum for reflection.

Building a supportive network

An important source of support which should not be neglected is having a good informal network. This means building working relationships with people within and outside your organisation. You can build a network up through joint working, serving on committees, socialising in breaks at meetings as well as being active within forums and social media. Early in my career as a social worker I carried out joint family work with an educational psychologist and served as the liaison member of staff with the local Barnardo's family centre. Taking up opportunities like this are excellent ways to grow as a social worker and find out about resources and services. The best approach is to be generous in helping other people and always to take a genuine interest in colleagues as professionals and as people. You should be honest, straightforward and helpful in your dealings with everyone you come into contact with regardless of their role and status or what they can do for you. Always take an interest in other people as human beings and reach out to a colleague who seems sad or troubled.

If you adopt this approach in your work you will never be short of help or support when you need it. By taking an interest in the work of other organisations you can also build up knowledge which will help you identify resources and sources of support for service users.

Chapter recap

In this chapter you were asked to reflect on what you thought the function of supervision was and what constituted good supervision. We reviewed the process of making a supervision contract, preparing for supervision and recording the outcomes from supervision. We spent some time considering what made supervision reflective and also how mindfulness could be used to improve the quality of supervision and ensure that we get the most benefit from it when we go back into practice. The chapter ended with a brief look at alternative models of support and the importance of developing professional networks.

Next up!

In the next chapter I will look at effective leadership and what it means to be a good team member. Different leadership styles will be considered and how effective they are in relation to different workplace issues. The psychology of working in teams and groups will be considered and how coaching good leadership can enhance team performance.

I also return to the concept of Lean management and look at how social work managers and staff can make their workplace more efficient, productive and stress-free through eliminating waste.

8

LEADING AND FOLLOWING FOR EFFECTIVE AND EFFICIENT PRACTICE

Key Concepts and Issues in this Chapter

- The unconscious life of teams
- Being a good team member
- Exercising influence in teams and groups
- Professional panics and professional curiosity
- Leadership theories – trait theories, behavioural theories, contingency theories and Taoist theories
- Participatory management
- Creating a positive organisational culture
- Lean management as a leadership tool in times of austerity
- The seven wastes in Lean
- Rapid Improvement events
- Distinguishing value added and non-value added activities
- Leadership for resilient organisations

This chapter will look at the importance of good leadership in achieving high quality practice and a safe and supportive team environment for workers. I will also consider what it means to be a good team member who supports their colleagues and is working towards the shared goals of the team and the organisation which it is part of.

Being part of a team

Whenever we go to a job interview there is likely to be a question about whether we are good at working in a team. The acceptable answer to those sorts of questions is that we love working as part of a team and that we are a good team member. Of course, not everyone does enjoy working closely with other people. Some people prefer to own a particular task or role and work quite independently. Some people enjoy coming together to work with other people on a project by project basis rather than always being part of the same team. However, expressing less than whole-hearted delight at the prospect of teamwork is to invite rejection. Ideally, employers want workers who are capable of working equally well independently and as part of a team. However, there can be aspects of working in teams which are sometimes contrary to effective or harmonious working. We looked at the problems of interpersonal conflict and bullying in Chapter 6. In this chapter we look in more depth at some issues around team work.

Our views about team working will be influenced by our previous experiences of being part of a team. Have we previously been part of teams where everyone does their share and helps out or have we been part of teams in which there has been interpersonal strife and unequal sharing of workload? From a psychodynamic perspective our earliest experience in being part of a group is when we are growing up as part of a family. It can therefore be argued that our experiences of being part of a family will influence how we interact in groups throughout the rest of our life. Problems such as sibling rivalry and oedipal conflicts can be mirrored in teams through disagreements between colleagues and challenges to the leader.

Bion and the group unconsciousness

Morgan and Thomas (1996) reviewed the work of Bion in applying psychodynamic theory to group dynamics in a workplace setting. Bion's concept of the group is that it can act positively as 'container' for negative feelings, in the same way as the mother/infant relationship does. However, the other side of this coin is that the infant is believed to have negative as well as positive emotions towards its carer as a result of feelings of dependency and helplessness and in a group setting these can be experienced as persecutory anxiety. Individuals can also experience anxiety about the loss of individuality which can occur in becoming part of a group.

Bion's most significant contribution to understanding group dynamics was his development of the concept of a 'group mentality' or 'group culture'. Bion carried out therapeutic group work with groups within an army psychiatric hospital after the Second World War. Bion concluded in his work that in any group there are two groups working: one is the work group which is serving the stated aim of the group. The other group, which consists of the same people, is the unconscious group (called a basic assumption group by Bion) which works to a hidden agenda which the group members are not normally aware of. Morgan and Thomas (1996) stated that Bion discovered that the hidden agenda in his groups of patients was a shared belief that the majority of patients were malingerers. Once this belief was identified then it could be challenged. Morgan and Thomas (1996: 73) stated that Bion believed that the unconscious group functioned to 'satisfy unconscious needs and defend against anxiety'. The problem with the unconscious group is that its aims and associated behaviours are often in conflict with what the group or team is really trying to achieve.

Exercise

Reflecting on Your Experiences in Groups and Teams

Think about your experiences of being part of a team. Are there any parallels between these experiences and your earlier experiences as a child or as an adult of being part of other teams, groups or families? Do you think your earlier experiences have contributed to your attitude to teams or the sorts of roles you play within them? Have you ever been in team or group situations where there have been behaviours which have negative consequences for the team as a whole or which work against improving the work of the team? What sort of purpose could these behaviours serve?

Being a positive member of a team

We are unlikely to get access to a therapist such as Bion to sort out interpersonal issues in a team we are part of. However, having an understanding of the possible influences of unconscious factors can give us patience and understanding about the motivations of others and the possibility that we are projecting conflicts and anxieties from elsewhere into our working relationships.

We all can strive to be a good and effective team member, even if team working is not our favourite way of working. Weinbach and Taylor (2011) suggest that good team members have three important qualities: self-management, job management and boss management. Self-management is the ability to maintain good relationships with colleagues, take responsibility for one's own feelings, and hold a positive view about one's employer and its objectives. Job management consists of good time management and an ability to meet objectives and deadlines. Boss management involves an understanding of the management style of one's manager and willingness to work cooperatively with them. Helping one's manager or team leader will help the overall performance of the team as well as maintain harmony and good working relationships. Workers have much closer contact with service users and with the problems and opportunities in the work environment. It is important that they use this knowledge to inform managers and team leaders about important issues which the team ought to consider.

Many of the answers to what makes a good team member can be found in a classic work by Dale Carnegie (2006); originally published in 1936 and subsequently revised, Carnegie's book *How to Win Friends and Influence People* contains a set of rules for developing and maintaining good relationships with others. These rules include: showing respect for other people's opinions, admitting to when we are wrong about something, and talking about our own mistakes before we point out other people's. Although written for people in sales and business, Carnegie's book, in a light and entertaining way, gives a lot of advice which is useful to social workers in dealing with colleagues and service users.

Exercising influence in teams

Social workers often find themselves in situations where a decision is going to be reached by a group, e.g. their social work team or members of a case conference. It is useful therefore to have some understanding of how groups come to make decisions and how these decisions differ from ones reached by people individually. Baron and Byrne (2003) suggest that consensus develops in groups by rules which they describe as social decision schemes. The most simple and obvious of these is the 'majority wins rule' in which the position which is initially adopted by the majority of the group members will be the one which prevails. Another 'scheme' is the 'truth wins rule' which suggests that the decision which is the most correct or appropriate will be recognised by the group as a result of discussion. The 'first shift rule' suggests that the group will tend to arrive at a decision consistent with the first shift in opinion. Baron and Byrne indicate that 80 per cent of decisions in groups can be accounted for by one of these rules.

Hogg and Vaughn (2013) discussed the phenomena of group polarisation. This is the finding that groups will tend to reach decisions which are more polarised than the mean of the position that all the group members would take individually. Thus, if the majority of workers involved in a case are tending towards a particular decision then the result of a case conference will be a commitment to this decision which is stronger than the average tendency of the group. Different reasons have been put forward for this tendency. One is the persuasive arguments theory. This argument suggests that if a number of members of the group favour a particular view then there are likely to be a number of good arguments brought forward for that view. People who already hold that viewpoint will have their views strengthened and made more polarised by hearing these views. Another perspective is social comparison theory. This suggests that people will develop a perspective which is socially valued by the group as a whole. Thus in a group of social workers, individual workers will be reluctant to express a view which is out of step with their peers. If they value the opinions of the group then they will go further towards the opinion which is approved of in the group so that they too will gain approval. A variation on this theory suggests that people who hold a particular opinion strongly may falsely believe that their opinion is extreme or out of touch. Once they find out that others share their opinion they may feel more liberated to express it. A third perspective, self-categorisation theory, holds that polarisation only occurs when the initial group tendency is interpreted as representing the norm for an 'in-group' (socially valued group members) rather than just an average opinion for the group as a whole. Thus, we may be especially influenced by other professionals who share perspectives which are valued by our profession.

The ways in which groups reach decisions are important because of the danger of the phenomenon known as groupthink. This was defined by Janis (1972) as being a way of thinking in which members of a particular group will subordinate the need for proper debate about important decisions to the need for group unanimity. Janis studied a variety of bad US policy decisions such as the Bay of Pigs invasion and found that a desire to conform and a lack of serious consideration of alternatives were features of those bad policy decisions. A more up-to-date example could be the UK's participation in the Iraq war. This was a situation in which there was strong political pressure on MPs and government agencies not to question a decision which had apparently been made in haste. At the same time there was a lack of tangible evidence to justify going to war. At the time of writing, the Chilcott Inquiry into the Iraq war is yet to deliver its verdict but it seems likely that the decision-making processes behind the war will be heavily criticised.

Groupthink and a failure to make solid independent judgements are an issue which social workers should be aware of. It is important in meetings and discussion forums to allow minority opinions to be expressed and considered. A leadership style which allows a range of concerns and issues to be considered is helpful in avoiding groupthink.

Moral panics

Sometimes a similar phenomenon to groupthink can be seen to operate at the level of a whole profession and this has sadly been a feature at times of social work, which has periodically been gripped by moral panics such as the Cleveland child abuse scandal. Cree et al. (2015: ix), in discussing moral panics stated that 'social work as an academic discipline and profession plays a central role in the process of defining social issues and then trying to do something about them... So we have to be particularly alert to the part we play within this'. Thus, social work has a responsibility in scrutinising evidence and forming judgements about the nature and extent of social problems on a sound basis. Furedi (2013: vii) stated that in a 'moral crisis' 'emotion is allowed far more latitude to influence matters than is the norm, and often incites responses that lack restraint and careful thought'.

I experienced one of these moral panics myself in my early days as a social worker in relation to ritual satanic abuse. The idea that large numbers of children were being ritually abused by practising Satanists was being circulated widely throughout the social work community in the late 1980s/early 1990s via seminars and even articles in respectable social work publications. Some colleagues were of the belief that large numbers of children were being satanically abused, often under the protection of corrupt figures in the police, judiciary and medical professions. I was informed by one senior colleague that young women were being impregnated in stately homes and their babies sacrificed in satanic rituals. Few people seemed to question the fact that there was no corroboration being offered for these claims or the fact that some of the people putting forward these claims were representatives of fringe religious organisations. Sadly, as with similar panics, the credulity of the social work profession in uncritically accepting these claims was detrimental to the reputation of the profession. LaFontaine (1994) in an extensive analysis of reports found no evidence of any cases in which there was evidence of satanic abuse. She found three cases where there had been an element of ritual but this had not been satanic and was secondary to the abuse itself. She found that disclosures of satanic elements had been influenced by adults.

One of the reasons I believe that moral panics can take hold in social work is because of the emotive nature of the subject matter. There was a reluctance to dismiss claims about satanic abuse because it was seen as dismissing the voices of victims. However, in the case of child victims the ritualistic connections appear to have been suggested by adults with poor interviewing skills. It is important that social workers retain a healthy scepticism, even in relation to emotive subject matters, while having a healthy curiosity about issues which may not yet have reached the public or professional consciousness.

Exercise

Reflecting on Moral Panics

Think about a moral panic or a scandal involving social work where people have quickly accepted information or allegations which have subsequently been found to be without foundation. What sort of questions do you think should have been asked before there was widespread acceptance that the concerns were well founded? Do you think that the moral panic would have taken hold if evidence had been more dispassionately explored?

Professional curiosity and courage

While it is important to avoid being swept up in moral panics it is equally important to be aware of dangers and problems which have not yet come into general awareness. The term for this is professional curiosity. Social work, together with the Police and other agencies have been slow and in some cases negligent in their response to recently recognised forms of child sexual exploitation such as street grooming. Oxfordshire Council were heavily criticised in a serious case review (Oxfordshire Safeguarding Children Board, 2015) for failing to recognise a pattern of organised abuse of 273 girls. Professionals were criticised for a lack of 'professional curiosity' and for using styles of language such as saying that girls were 'prostituting themselves' which put the blame for the abuse on the victims. There have been cases of large-scale grooming by gangs across a number of UK cities in the past few years and, sadly, a similar pattern in which abuse of young people has been dismissed as being a 'lifestyle choice' rather than a crime. The very nature of social work, as a profession which works with people in their communities, means that social workers are likely to be among the first professionals to identify new patterns of abuse or exploitation.

In the case of street grooming in Rotherham the government report by Louise Casey said that child protection services were very much 'framed within the context of inter-familial abuse' and that 'expertise, procedures, systems and resources tend[ed] to reflect that context' (Casey, 2015: 42). Street abuse was a phenomenon which fell outside the pattern of abuse which child protection services had been geared to tackling. Being able to identify and address this new pattern of abuse required an ability to think outside of existing attitudes and procedures. It also requires a culture in which professional curiosity is encouraged and supported by management and where staff who want to raise uncomfortable or difficult issues are empowered to do so.

Exercise

What Does Professional Curiosity Mean to You?

The term 'professional curiosity' has been used a lot recently in situations where social work failures have been identified. Think about what the term means to you and try to come up with a definition for it. How do you think professional curiosity can be fostered and supported in social work? What are the roles of individual social workers and managers in achieving this?

Driving positive change through good leadership

I'd like to shift our thinking now on to the concept of leadership and what makes a good leader in social work.

Exercise

What Makes a Good Leader?

Spend 15 minutes thinking about what qualities, behaviours and strategies you think a good leader might have. It might help to think about experiences which you have had directly of good leadership. Hopefully you will have some examples, but if this doesn't help then think about figures you have heard of from politics or business whom you believe to be good leaders. Make a list of these qualities, behaviours and strategies.

Now reflect on your list. Is your list made up of mainly personal qualities or mainly behaviours? Are the different elements consistent with each other or are some of them contradictory? Do you think all of the elements would work in all circumstances or all situations or with all types of people? Do you think some people are natural leaders or do you think leadership is a skill like any other which can be developed through experience?

Leadership theories

The idea that there could be a set of qualities which define a good leader was a feature of the earliest theories about leadership. These are referred to as trait theories – the view that there are sets of characteristics which single out leaders from other people. This approach can be traced back to Thomas Carlyle's (1849) analysis of 'great men' who had helped shape history. The problem with many trait theories is that they contain very long lists of qualities. I imagine your list may have contained a lot of positive qualities which you want from a leader, but which are a tall order for one person to fulfil when taken together. Zaccaro et al. (2004) came up with a more integrated approach in which different types of traits around personality, social skills and cognitive abilities work in combination to enable someone to emerge as a good leader in the workplace. It is the interaction of these different traits which results in good leadership.

It may be that the leadership qualities list that you created had a fair number of behaviours. Theories in which the behaviours rather than the disposition of the leader is the most important factor are called, unsurprisingly, behavioural leadership theories.

One example of a behavioural leadership style theory is 'Theory X and Theory Y' developed by McGregor (McGregor, 1960). Basically this approach suggests that what is important is the leader's attitude to other people and their own internal psychological theories about what motivates other people. People with what McGregor calls Theory X will have a fundamental belief that workers only respond to rewards and punishments and that these need to be applied to get effective performance. Theory Y people have a more humanistic orientation to other people in the workplace and believe that people will naturally want to do the best job that they can.

Managers with this more positive outlook will be encouraging and trusting towards staff whereas those holding Theory X will be more controlling and distrustful. Of course, it is likely that most leaders will have elements of both these perspectives. The leader's attitudes will affect the followers' approach to work and leaders may shift their attitudes depending on the attitudes and approach to work of the workers.

Behavioural leadership theories have developed into an approach which is generally referred to as leadership style theories. It is important to note that these different categories of leadership theory are not mutually exclusive. Transformational leadership theory is a theory which includes a focus on traits and behaviours. The concept of transformational leadership was originally developed by James Burns (2012), a Presidential biographer, and refined as a psychological theory by Bass and Riggio (2006). Transformational leaders are highly charismatic people who use their personality, vision and communication skills to lead people inspirationally and bring about great change. Transformational leaders have been found to score high for the personality traits of extraversion, openness to experience, agreeableness and conscientiousness and score low for neuroticism. Transformational leaders are able to generate loyalty and commitment in their followers. Examples of transformational leaders are Margaret Thatcher, Tony Blair, Steve Jobs, Martin Luther King and Bill Gates. Those individuals have brought about huge change. However, it is very difficult to keep up the momentum which is needed to continue to keep followers inspired and there is a danger that individual workers can feel that their role is not important. There is also the danger of a vacuum being left and the vision being lost after the transformational leader steps down, as happened when Tony Blair stepped down as leader of the Labour Party.

A third approach to understanding what makes good leaders is what is called contingency theory. This approach to understanding leadership suggests that the best approach to leadership is dependent on the nature of the environment which the organisation is having to operate in. If we think about the case of a social services department, periods of reform and restructuring may favour a transformational leadership to successfully change the organisational culture.

Stogdill (1974) developed a contingency theory in which there were two axes of behaviour – consideration (concern for staff wellbeing, offering encouragement, etc.) and structure (monitoring of budgets, targets and deadlines). Rather than one axis of behaviour being more important than the other, Stogdill was of the view that different situations require a different approach. In social work terms, periods of austerity may favour a more rigid bureaucratic style to ensure that the department stays within budgetary restrictions. Conversely, where there are large amounts of emotional stress from working on a series of distressing or difficult cases, consideration may be a more important quality in a leader.

Taoist theory of leadership

Michael LaTorra (1993) produced a modern version of the *Tao Te Ching*. This is a spiritual book written by Lao Tzu in ancient China in the 6th century BC, which has been translated and re-interpreted many times. LaTorra was a scientific writer with an interest in technology and is now an academic. His interpretation of the Tao is I believe a very useful document for anyone trying to maintain a sense of calm and purpose in a very busy and complex world. The teachings are entirely compatible with developing a mindful approach and with being a reflective practitioner. There is a great deal of wisdom on every page, though one of the most helpful passages for me is in his definition of good leadership: 'The best leader guides, he does not govern... He works in the background. His objective is to make himself obsolete' (LaTorra, 1993: 35). There is part of being a manager that does involve giving instructions or commands. However, this is not the part of the job in which the real leadership actually occurs. Rather, leadership occurs through inspiring and enabling others.

I think the idea that a good leader works in the background is also very important. No matter how good a leader is they cannot do all the elements of the job themselves. They are dependent on others to do most of the work. This will only happen if the team has a role in developing strategies and takes ownership of them. Workers also have to get credit for their labour and commitment. A manager who seeks to take credit for all the achievements of his/her team will quickly lose their respect and loyalty. The same applies to someone who uses leadership skills to promote a new or innovative form of practice. If other people do not take ownership of the new working methods and begin to take pride in them, then they will quickly disappear again once the promotional initiative has ended. A good leader is someone who makes others feel good about their own work and does not seek fame for themselves.

Of course we all know people who appear to have got ahead in life through self-promotion. However, if you think for a few minutes you will realise that they usually have lots of detractors and people who are waiting for them to fail. If, on the other hand, people give credit where it is due and inspire and support others then they will be repaid in co-operation and help when they need it. This is what leadership is really about.

Exercise

Your Role as a Leader

Take a little time to reflect on what elements of your job involve management or leadership. If you are not in a management role, then reflect on how you are able to show leadership and promote good practice in your job. If you are in a management role then reflect on how much of your role actually involves inspiring and guiding others and praising good practice as opposed to the routine elements of management. Then think about how you could be a more inspirational leader.

Participatory management and consultation

Pine and Healy (2007) quoted a statement by Jack Welch, an American CEO, which gives a similar message to the Taoist perspective. Welch said that 'You're only as good as the reflected glory you get from the work of your people. Management isn't you doing it. Management is exciting others to do it better than you ever could have done it.' Pine and Healy suggest a participatory management style in which workers are given a role in making organisational decisions. They state that this is increasingly important in an environment of rapid change. Social services departments are quite hierarchical organisations. However, there are opportunities to carry out genuine consultation on organisational issues and involve staff in redesigning services and making operational decisions. It is vital when management consultation exercises are carried out that staff are told the true extent of what they can influence as opposed to what is non-negotiable. If staff feel that they are being asked about things which have already been decided then this will erode trust and lead to a perception that the whole consultation has been a sham. A proper consultation should be a **dialogue** which **leads** to a decision.

Creating a good organisational climate

Weinbach and Taylor (2011) set out some of the key variables that are important to a good organisational climate. They include an understanding and appreciation of the importance of good team work. Creating a climate of co-operation is essential to achieving this. It is important for team leaders to show fairness to all team members and not play favourites or set up situations in which people will develop mistrust or rivalries. Good communication is important in achieving this. It is important that staff receive important information which affects them promptly and through appropriate channels. Another factor which Weinbach and Taylor identify is a clear understanding by team members of what each other's roles are. The leader or manager must make it clear what does and does not fall within their own role and similarly the roles of their staff. Weinbach and Taylor also state the importance of social work managers in advocating for their staff. It is important in situations such as excessive work pressures or staff shortages for the team leader to be an advocate for the team and negotiate with senior management to resolve such issues.

Social work is a skilled job in which considerable creativity, independent thought and initiative are needed. A good leader should therefore cultivate a climate where team members feel that they are trusted professionals who can take as much responsibility as possible for how they carry out their work. It is therefore important to avoid micro-management or make staff reluctant to use their initiative. This has of course to be balanced with a need to ensure that staff are adhering to organisational policies and procedures and the law. Weinbach and Taylor stated that a good leader will try to ensure an environment of mutual respect and confidence as the basis for an effective team.

Leadership in times of austerity

Effective leadership is always important but especially in times of austerity where there is the need to maintain high standards while at the same time saving resources. In this second half of the chapter I want to look at the role that Lean management can play in achieving this.

Lean management

As we discussed in a previous chapter, Lean management is a method of service improvement which has been developed in the private sector and which was pioneered by the Toyota Motor Company. It has been embraced enthusiastically by the UK's National Health Service, which now employs many Lean practitioners. Sadly, there has not been the same level of enthusiasm in local government and very little recognition of it in social work.

An important principle in Lean is the identification and elimination of waste. According to the principles of Lean there are seven types of waste commonly found. Normally those are described in ways which relate to industrial processes but Black and Miller (2008) showed Lean of principles could be adapted to health care settings. I will now describe the different forms of waste within the Lean model by adapting the Black and Miller list to social work.

The seven wastes in Lean and how they are manifested in social work

1. Over-production

This is where a greater number of outputs are produced than is needed or work is done to a much higher standard than is necessary. This is a huge problem in social work. I frequently hear social workers telling me that they prepare long and verbose reports for meetings, case conferences, etc. only to be asked at the meeting to give a bullet point summary. Clearly there is important information which has to go into reports. However, there is lots of information which finds its way into reports just because it is traditional to include it or because of a house style for reports, or because professionals are anxious about leaving information out. It is generally believed that a full and comprehensive report is a good one. Of course, more information is always helpful. However, there will always come a point at which the marginal cost of collecting and reporting additional information outweighs the benefit. It is often only when managers have to pay for something out of their budget that it makes them think about whether they really need it. I will give an example from my early experience in social work. At this time the local authority which I worked for owned its own care homes. Prior to admission of a resident a request was sent to the service user's GP (physician) for a report on the state of their health. There were two rates for reports. The charge for a report from existing case notes was £40. However, if the local authority wanted a more in-depth report based on a fresh examination then the charge would be £80. My manager told me that I should always request the £40 report. She said that she would like the longer report but that the local authority could not afford it. She thought that it was wrong for the GP to ask for more money to write the longer report. I said that I agreed with the GP's policy. Think for a minute about why I might think that. If the GP charged the same amount for the longer report then they would always be asked for one. This would take away time which they use for caring for patients and their other duties. Clearly the short reports were 'good enough' otherwise the local authority would pay the extra money for the long reports. Now imagine what would happen if the GPs were directly employed by the local authority rather than being self-employed. Most likely they would have been spending lots of time writing long reports for managers and complaining about not having enough time for patients.

It is the capacity of markets for allocating resources effectively that is the motivation for bringing market principles into public sector organisations. The theory is that market discipline and market forces will lead to more efficient services. However, public sector organisations are not the same as private businesses. There are inherent difficulties in trying to import the principles of the private sector to the public sector. When a private business fails the losses fall on the shareholders or owners. When a department in a hospital or a public sector body loses its contracts then it is the taxpayer who is responsible for the redundancy or restructuring costs. Yanis Varoufakis (former Greek finance Minister) speaking on *Question Time* (24 September 2015) stated that the UK had become obsessed with market fetishisation in which markets were being brought into areas where a genuine free market cannot operate.

There is a viable alternative to marketisation for dealing with waste in the public sector. By using Lean management we can identify waste from over-production within our own organisation without the need for internal markets. We do this by being ready to question the value of every aspect of every activity we do in our job. The question should not be whether it is better to do B than A but whether the additional time and labour involved in doing B provides more value than whatever else we could have done with the same resources. The most worthwhile alternative use is known in cost accounting terms as the opportunity cost. This is the benefit which we are sacrificing to perform the task. Thus, when we are determining whether producing a long report rather than a short one amounts to over-production then we need to balance the additional value produced against the opportunity cost. In social work terms the opportunity cost of writing a longer report might be doing an initial visit to a service user who has been waiting several weeks to have their case allocated. If a short report is good enough then we might choose to opt for that and allow workers to use the time saved to clear unallocated cases.

2. Waste of time on hand (waiting)

This can occur for two groups of people – service users and workers. Facilities and processes which are not fit for purpose cause great frustration for workers and cause unacceptable waste of time for them. Many social workers who have to use hot desking have complained about travelling to hot desking sites only to find that there are no desks available or that other staff, who are absent, have 'taken ownership' of the desks (an IT equivalent of putting towels on sun beds). One way of dealing with availability which has been tried is to use an app that tells staff where the nearest available desk is at any given time. Education on hot desking etiquette is also helpful. Staff are a hugely expensive resource so it is a false economy to stint on adequate IT and support systems. Most readers who work in social care will have experience of unnecessary delays due to inefficient IT or waiting for resources. Examples of unnecessary waiting for service users could be a delay in having their case allocated. Now, most local authorities have a team with a name like 'intake team' or 'customer services'. This team will resolve simple queries or signpost people to other services or resources. This means that people with easily resolved problems do not have to wait to be allocated to social workers in busy teams. Any improvement which reduces delays for service users is going to be helpful.

3. Waste of inventory

We do not normally think of social care as being a service which has 'inventory'. However, social workers do use consumables such as stationery, pens, etc. A frequent source of waste in organisations in which I have worked has occurred whenever there was a change in corporate logo. Whenever this happened large amounts of headed paper had to be destroyed. A feature of Lean management is to have what is called kanbans. These are ways of signalling when we need more inventory. It ensures that we don't run out of something important or alternatively stock up too much on something which then becomes redundant before we can use it. If you see a product in a shop which is displayed on a peg you will often come across a label which says order more stock. The label is placed just at the right point to trigger the retailer to order additional stock. It is a low cost but highly effective method of stock control. As a social worker you can make your own kanbans to alert you to when you have to do reports or reviews of service users. You can do this by using Outlook calendar to generate reminders for you when you need to start preparing for a review of a service user or begin writing a report. If you manage these predictable demands on your workload then you can work ahead of your deadlines and avoid being overwhelmed by conflicting demands near to the date a report is due. Another source of inventory which is highly expensive is over-supply of residential places or the wrong type of places. This has been a problem in the past because of a lack of information for providers on what types of services are going to be needed. One of the responsibilities given to local authorities by the Care Act is to carry out social care market shaping. This is not something that local authorities have traditionally been good at. When I worked as a mental health social worker I used to be asked by care businesses for my views about what sort of care facilities might be needed on my patch in the future based on current trends. I was always willing to answer questions like this because I thought that by doing so I could improve future service provision and keep suppliers afloat. This opinion was not shared by many colleagues, however, as there has long been a great deal of suspicion and hostility towards the private sector in social work. The new requirement of market shaping will force local authorities to take some responsibility for ensuring that adequate and appropriate services are available in their locality. This will require strategic thinking and a more positive attitude towards partnership working with the private and voluntary sectors.

4. Waste of movement

This is where people or resources are moved unnecessarily. Examples of this include people having to travel to the other side of a building to find a photocopier or printer. It should be considered, however, that for sedentary workers such as social workers a certain amount of movement during the day can be useful in terms of people maintaining fitness. It is a health benefit for social workers to walk as much as possible during their working day and to get up and move around frequently rather than working solidly for hours at a computer screen without any physical activity. Using stairs rather than an elevator is also a good way to exercise. Movement can be good but this should be as a result of a positive decision to exercise rather than a poorly planned office environment.

5. Waste in transportation

If we were talking about a factory-type setting this would refer to unnecessary transportation of goods. In social work we can think of this in terms of unnecessary transportation of social workers. Travelling between locations takes time and causes expensive use of fuel and carbon emissions. Examples of this could be social workers attending meetings at locations far from their office or patch or having to travel to offices to do case recording. We now have technologies such as Skype with which to communicate with colleagues or have virtual meetings or teleconferences. We can also facilitate remote access to case recording provided concerns about information security can be successfully resolved.

6. Waste of defective products

This refers to processing mistakes, which cost time and resources to put right. In a local authority this can involve errors in case recording, letters sent out to the wrong person or the wrong address. In social work these errors can be catastrophic. In an office in which I once worked sensitive confidential information was sent in error to someone whom it was not intended for. This led to a serious breach of confidentiality and consequences for service user trust in the authority. Data breaches such as this should be avoided at all costs and it is worth investing time and energy in developing systems to reduce the likelihood of errors of this nature.

7. Waste in processing

This involves unnecessary reworking of completed work or the repetition of data entry. This is the category of waste which is perhaps the most significant in social work. Even when visionary local authorities supply workers with tablet computers, many social workers insist on writing information on paper then redrafting it on paper and then only finally typing it when they are sure it is exactly as they want it. A good rule to follow is that you should only ever write something once. Having once typed something onto a computer or other electronic device, then you can edit it, correct it, expand upon it, condense it, copy it into another document, etc. Writing the same information multiple times in different media and different formats is wasteful of time. Another waste of resources is printing reports and other information off before reading them. Printing off reports for service users to read is a useful thing to do, but social workers and other professionals should be able to read their reports electronically. If you are inviting other professionals to a meeting or case conference, if you can, send them the report electronically in advance and leave the responsibility of printing off a paper copy if they require one to them. This will save time for you in printing and collating.

Exercise

Identifying Waste

Choose a process which you know well in your organisation e.g. the processing of a social work referral. Think about all the steps which occur between the initial enquiry being made and the conclusion of the assessment. Consider all the forms and other documents which are created and processed. Try to identify as many examples as you can of the seven wastes during this process.

Kaizen Events

Lean has much wider applications than just identifying single instances of waste. It can also be used to analyse and improve whole systems.

The key to improving services within a Lean approach is to reduce the number of tasks or activities which are 'non-value added'. These are stages or actions in processes which do not contribute to the experience of the customer or service user. Some tasks which are non-value added are nevertheless essential to the service being provided. One example of this is activities associated with monitoring spending. Clearly, systems for recording and monitoring spending are needed otherwise money would run out before the end of the financial year and the authority would be unable to meet the needs of people with urgent care needs. Case recording and report writing are tasks which have value added, non-value added (essential) and non-value added (unnecessary) components. The value added element is in the fact that recording and sharing information improves multi-disciplinary working, and can facilitate access to resources for the service user. The non-value added (essential) component is derived from the importance of records as a way of maintaining a permanent record of what social work decisions have been taken in addition to recording important incidents in the lives of service users. For example, recording of key incidents and areas of concern in a child care case are essential. Non-value added (unnecessary) components would include any duplication of recording such as having to record the same information in different electronic systems which do not communicate with each other.

The aim of Lean management is to reduce the number of activities which are both non-value added and unnecessary. The formal way of doing this within Lean is to hold what is called a Rapid Improvement Workshop, a Kaizen Event or sometimes a Kaizen Blitz. In this type of event all of the people involved in an activity come together for a day and map out every step of the process. This is often done on post-it labels on a blank wall. Each post-it will have a step in the process written on it. When this process is done you end up with what looks like a very large flow chart on the wall. Once it is done each step in the process is identified as value added, non-value added (essential) or non-value added (unnecessary). By examining a process in depth, stage by stage, in this manner we can redesign the process to eliminate unnecessary stages. This will save staff time, reduce waiting time for service users and remove frustration for everyone involved.

To carry out a Kaizen Event effectively you should receive training from an accredited teacher in Lean, a Master or Sensei. Carrying out a Kaizen Event also requires buy-in and commitment from the colleagues who will be implementing the new procedure. The purpose of the Kaizen Blitz is to bring together representatives of everyone involved in the process so that all the information and all the different perspectives have been taken into account in redesigning the process. If, however, you don't have this training or the resources to run a Kaizen Event you can still as a manager (or a worker, with support) review a process yourself and apply Kaizen principles.

Exercise

Distinguishing Between Value Added
and Non-value Added Stages

Return to the process which you considered during the exercise on identifying waste in the previous section. Now think more deeply about the different stages in the process and put each stage in the process into the categories of value added, non-value added (essential) and non-value added (unnecessary). Can you think of how the process could be changed to eliminate non-value added (unnecessary) stages and make the process run more efficiently and deliver better results for service users?

Lean as a mental attitude

It is a source of great frustration to me that concepts such as Lean management are dismissed by some writers as being examples of 'managerialism'. This is occurring at the same time that the social work media is full of accounts of social workers spending disproportionate amounts of time on admin tasks. If you are a social work manager, Lean is one of the most useful tools which you can use to improve the morale and effectiveness of your staff. There is unlikely to be more money and resources made available for social work in the short to medium term so improving efficiency is the only way we can relieve pressure on social workers.

Lean is a way of thinking and indeed a way of life. It is a mindful state. It involves being alert at all times to waste and being conscious about the degree to which the way we do our job is adding meaningful value to the people we are trying to help. For managers it is also about ensuring that the structures and processes of your organisation are helpful to your workers in performing their jobs effectively.

Leadership for resilient organisations

I would argue that for an organisation to be resilient it needs to foster the sort of creativity and dynamism which allows it to respond to changing and challenging circumstances while providing a supportive environment which protects staff from undue stress. Amabile and Khaire (2008) argued that organisations cannot manage creativity but rather they should 'manage *for* creativity'. This involves harnessing the imagination and abilities of all staff, providing intellectual challenge and utilising as diverse a range of perspectives as possible. It involves encouraging collaboration, getting ideas from outside the organisation and helping people to find ways through bureaucratic obstacles to their ideas. They noted that it is important that improving efficiency does not lead people to focus too restrictively on existing processes at the expense of thinking about more fundamental changes which their organisation might need to make. They gave the example of Kodak, which had kept trying to improve the manufacture of film rather than respond to the new technologies of digital photography. In social work terms, with developments such as direct payments and increasing responsibilities in relation to safeguarding, the nature of the social work task is changing and models used for providing social work services will have to respond to these changes.

Wiseman and McKeown (2010) stated that good leaders are 'multipliers' who take the time to understand and recognise where their team members' talents are. They foster a productive environment in which people feel able to generate ideas and use their own judgement. When they delegate tasks, they let workers own their work, take responsibility for it and take credit for it.

Spreitzer and Porath (2012) emphasised the importance of leaders sharing information with all employees and ensuring that they all understood the policies and missions of the organisation. There is much greater awareness of this in social services organisations nowadays. Briefings on developments such as the Care Act are given to all staff including admin staff and unqualified workers so that everyone understands the implications of the new responsibilities and duties.

Organisations also need to take responsibility for the stress faced by employees and actively encourage good habits like getting exercise and dealing with stress positively. One of the local authorities in my area for example has a display of leaflets with short relaxing walks that can quickly take employees out of the urban environment to connect with nature for short spells over lunchtime. Organisations can also encourage running, cycling and other activities during the working day.

Cryer et al. (2003) outlined a stress management process which staff can be taught called freeze frame. This is useful where people are habitually adopting a fight or flight response to their environment as a result of ongoing and protracted exposure to stress. The first stage in this process is actually recognising the physical and psychological symptoms of the onset of a stressful or irritable reaction and making a commitment to take time out from it. This should help us to realise that we need to relax and disengage from the thing which is stressing us. The next stage is called 'breathing through your heart'. This involves focusing on the area near the heart and inhaling for five seconds and then exhaling for five seconds while visualising breath going out through the solar plexus. At the same we should try to visualise something positive such as being somewhere which we have a good feeling about or being with people we love. We should try to engage all the senses in our imagination. For example, we could imagine being on the beach on holiday with our partner and hearing the waves, smelling the ocean, feeling the sun on our body, etc. Once we have calmed ourselves in this we can then try to think objectively about a different way to handle the situation which initially made us feel stressed. When we have achieved this we should reflect on how differently we feel about having reduced our stress and having a different perspective on our situation. With repetition we should be able to develop new, more positive ways of habitually responding to difficult situations other than going into a fight or flight response. The authors claim that this breathing pattern modulates the heart rhythm and replaces the chaotic rhythms caused by negative emotions with more positive regular ones. This practice can also be done when one anticipates stressful meetings or interactions in order to approach these situations more positively.

Chapter recap

In this chapter we looked at what it means to be a member of a team. Psychodynamic ideas were introduced to look at how unconscious dynamics can influence the psychological life of teams. We looked at how we can be a good team member before moving on to look at ways in which we can influence others and simultaneously maintain professional curiosity and a healthy scepticism.

We then looked at different theories about what makes a good leader and the role of leaders in creating a positive organisational climate.

The second half of the chapter was concerned with how Lean management theory can be used to improve efficiency in difficult economic circumstances.

Further study

If you want to understand more about how people function in groups and teams then a good introductory text in social psychology is a good start which will then give you the concepts which you will need to read papers which are based in psychological theory.

If you want to find out more about Lean management then I would recommend doing a training course run by a reputable provider.

Next up!

In the next chapter I will bring together different threads from the rest of the book and focus on how you can build a resilient career going forward.

9

CHOOSING MINDFUL PRACTICE AND BUILDING A RESILIENT CAREER

Key Concepts and Issues in this Chapter

- Joyful effort
- Mindful careers
- Emotional intelligence and resilience
- Reality testing
- Flexibility
- Impulse control
- Happiness
- Optimism
- Developing emotional agility
- Developing creative thinking skills
- Managing career transitions
- Dealing with setbacks and disappointments
- Intelligent CV creation
- Your CV as a source of job security
- Future impacts of new technologies
- Managing your future

Introduction

Historian Edward Gibbon (1776) said, 'The winds and the waves are always on the side of the ablest navigators.' What Gibbon was saying is that there is no good or bad luck but rather that people who are skilled and competent can effectively steer themselves through the treacherous waters of difficult times. I introduced this idea in Chapter 2 when I gave the example of Derren Brown's programme in which he found that people with a more positive, open approach were able to take advantage of opportunities when they became available. Social workers who are finishing their training now are beginning their career in an environment of great change and significant challenge. Local authorities are facing financial restrictions as never before while the Care Act has increased their responsibilities. There is no easy prescription for what social workers can do to ensure that they have a rewarding career in which they achieve real change for those that they serve but in this chapter I will consider some of what can be done in this respect.

Joyful effort in work

Social work requires an approach which Buddhists might refer to as joyful effort – that is, a striving to do a good job while obtaining pleasure and fulfilment from the work. The Dalai Lama and Howard Cutler (2003) discussed three different approaches to how we can regard work: as a way of earning money, as a way of building a career or as a 'calling' which serves a higher purpose. They suggested that while we might think intuitively that certain jobs would lend themselves to this way of thinking more than others, this is not always the case. They used examples to illustrate that some people can achieve joy and fulfilment in relatively routine jobs whereas some people in what ought to be more meaningful jobs can become burnt out and disillusioned. Reminding ourselves of the importance of the work which we do and how it helps people is important when we begin to feel disillusioned by the frustrations of the workplace. It may be that sometimes when we are feeling brought down by bureaucracy and lack of resources we have to focus on the smaller things we have achieved which have been beneficial to others. For example, answering an email query from a colleague might seem a small achievement. However, if we were able to direct them to a resource which was helpful to a service user then our small action may have achieved a significant benefit for another person. Celebrating small victories in stressed times is one way of staying engaged with what we are doing and avoiding descending into despair and burnout.

Building a mindful career

I introduced the concept of mindfulness in Chapter 2 as a technique for trying to see the world more clearly. At the beginning of Chapter 3 I suggested that one can easily lose track of one's purpose in relation to work. Here I want to argue that having mindfulness in relation to your middle- and long-term goals is important in terms of keeping your career on track. The reader might challenge me at this point on the usefulness of mindfulness as a tool in looking at where we are going in the longer term. After all, mindfulness is about being able to focus on the present. However, one of the reasons that people are thought to lack mindfulness is that they have a tendency to ruminate on the past and focus too much on future problems that might never occur (Shonin et al. 2015). By being mindful and being more aware of how we are feeling in the present we can think about how we feel about our longer-term career in a clearer and more realistic way. We can ensure that we are able to listen to our own thoughts and feelings without being overtaken by unnecessary fears or preoccupations.

If you want to develop mindfulness then you could consider joining a class or reading about how to practise mindfulness meditation. Mindfulness meditations usually involve focusing on the passage of the breath in and out of the body while intrusive thoughts are allowed to drift out of the mind. They involve letting go of distractions and preoccupations and opening the mind to peace and understanding. By clearing the mind we can be open to new experience and become more creative and in tune with our real selves.

Langer (2014) suggested that mindfulness can reduce stress by allowing us to escape from pessimistic or doom-laden predictions about how things will turn out. It can also prevent us from falling victim to the delusion that we are indispensable and solely responsible for the success or failure of any particular piece of work. By having a realistic appraisal of a situation we can approach it in a calmer and more logical way. There are several different ways in which most situations can be resolved, each of which will result in a different set of challenges and opportunities. Langer stated that the only situation in which mindfulness is not helpful is one in which we have found the very best way of doing something and also that nothing else changes. Of course, we are never likely to find ourselves in a situation where our life and our work are not changing. As I will discuss in this chapter, political and social change and the rapid development of technology mean that social work jobs are changing very quickly. By developing our career mindfully we can try to maintain our awareness of these changes while keeping in touch with our own personal and professional objectives.

The role of emotional intelligence in developing a resilient career

The concept of emotional intelligence has been much discussed in psychology over the past few decades. It has been developed as a concept to explain why some people appear to be better than others at understanding their own and other people's emotional states and utilising these insights to enhance their relationships. It is a highly controversial subject with some academics claiming that it is measuring a distinct and valid group of abilities which can predict job success while others dispute these claims. Locke (2005) questioned whether emotional intelligence is a distinct form of intelligence or simply an ability to apply intelligence effectively in the interpersonal domain. Another criticism has been that since emotional intelligence strongly correlates with certain personality traits, then it is these personality traits (plus general intelligence), rather than a distinct form of intelligence that is being measured by EI Inventories (Schulte et al., 2004). Landy (2005) reviewed the evidence for emotional intelligence as a predictor of work success and concluded that much of the evidence for this has come from outside mainstream science and cannot therefore be substantiated. It should be pointed out that creating measures for predicting success in business is a highly profitable industry. We should therefore be cautious in accepting at face value some of the bold claims which are often made about the value of psychometric tests. Some universities are at the moment contemplating whether to test students for emotional resilience before they come on to programmes. I would urge caution as the ability of psychometric tests to validly measure traits or skills which can be predictive of future success is open to question. I think it is more useful to apply knowledge from psychology to help people to develop their potential rather than to make judgements about their capabilities.

Whether we accept that emotional intelligence is a valid concept and something distinct from general intelligence and personality we can still accept that qualities associated with the construct are useful in promoting good interpersonal relationships at work.

Stein and Book (2006) described the Bar-On measure of emotional intelligence. This consists of 15 factors which they considered to be linked to success at work and how they could be developed. I would like to consider five of these factors: reality testing, flexibility, impulse control, happiness and optimism. I have chosen to focus on these factors because I consider that they are related to mindfulness and to building up resilience across the span of one's career.

Emotional intelligence: Reality testing

Reality testing was described by Stein and Book (2006: 173) as 'tuning in to the immediate situation'. It involves being able to arrive at an objective understanding of a situation and being able to test how accurate this is. This is not as straightforward an ability as it might seem. It is possible for two people to be confronted with exactly the same situation and reach very different conclusions about it. Freeman et al. (2005) demonstrated this using a virtual reality experiment. Participants wore headsets which immersed them in a virtual reality environment in which they would encounter other electronically generated people who might look at them or look away. The virtual reality characters were created to be neutral in the reactions towards the experimental subjects. However, even though all participants experienced the same visual stimuli, the way in which they interpreted the virtual reality characters varied greatly. Some participants thought they were friendly and welcoming, whereas others found them hostile or threatening. The degree to which the characters were found hostile or friendly correlated with participants' scores on the Fenigstein Paranoia scale. This is a measure of paranoia (suspicion about the intentions of others) across the non-clinical population. Paranoia score was positively correlated with making negative interpretations about the VR avatars. People with a tendency towards suspicion about other people in general would be more likely to see the virtual reality characters as threatening, whereas people who scored low for paranoia might see the same characters as being friendly or welcoming. What the study showed was that people's preconceptions about how trustworthy other people are has an influence on how they interpret social signals in their environment. There is obviously some benefit in being a little cautious about other people so that we can avoid danger. However, too much suspicion about others will make it difficult for us to make friends and get the most out of social interactions.

An ability to think objectively and reality test our social encounters is a skill which will help us to build our social network and establish good relationships with those that we work with. Stein and Book (2006: 173) state that this is the ability to 'discern the difference between the way things are and the way that we hope or fear they are'. It involves searching for evidence in the environment and then testing any interpretations which we come up with. This ability allows us to detect threats and problems quickly and avoid panicking unnecessarily and also to take advantage of opportunities as they arise.

Just as our psychological view of the world affects our interpretations and responses to social interactions, so too can our worldview affect our attitude to risks and opportunities in our work environment more generally. If we can develop a habit of carrying out reality testing when we encounter new situations rather than defaulting to either catastrophising or ignoring new information then we can respond to new situations in a mindful way. We can thus build resilience into our approach to work.

Exercise

Reality Testing

1. Think about a situation in which you got very upset and panicky and imagined a catastrophic outcome but for which the end result was satisfactory. Now think about why you jumped to conclusions about how bad things would get. What information did you use to arrive at the negative conclusion? What other information could you have taken into account to form a more balanced view? Why do you think you failed to arrive at a balanced perspective?

2. Now repeat the exercise with a situation in which you failed to react to important information and this resulted in an error or oversight. Was there an alternative way you could have responded? What steps could you take to respond more appropriately if a similar situation re-occurred?

3. Thinking about your responses to 1 and 2 above can you think of a strategy for ensuring you respond calmly but proportionately to important information about work?

Emotional intelligence: Flexibility

Stein and Book (2006) considered flexibility to be 'an ability to adjust emotions, thoughts and behaviours to changing situations and conditions'. They also stated that people with flexibility were 'open and tolerant of different ideas, orientations, ways and practices' (p.151).

Social work does of course need a great deal of flexibility. No two days in social work are exactly the same. Social workers frequently have to deal with unexpected crises and sometimes several at once. Anyone who requires a predictable environment for work is unlikely to find many jobs in social work which are suitable for them. However, social workers are also having to demonstrate flexibility in relation to the tools and structure of their work as well as the work itself. Technology and social policy are moving faster than they ever have. At the time I graduated as a social worker in 1989 my classmates and I expected that we would be doing a job that would last us our whole career until retirement and would probably not change much in that time. Current social work students are under no illusions that their job role will have this longevity. They are aware that they may have to face privatisation, outsourcing or possibly setting up their own independent practice. They are also aware that they will have to adapt to all sorts of technological changes in their work. Only very basic IT literacy was needed when I graduated and most typing and data entry were done by admin staff. This is an exceptional situation now and social workers must become increasingly adept at using new technology. Technological changes will have huge benefits in the long term but it requires all social workers to rapidly change their work practices. The changes in employment of social workers will create a great deal of uncertainty and instability for workers including fears about maintaining a regular and dependable income. Social workers will have to become accustomed to dealing with a rapidly changing environment.

Flexibility is something we can practise and develop. Many of our self-defeating habits such as procrastinating or over-eating are part of entrenched and habitual patterns of behaviour. By varying how we approach our day we can help ourselves break out of habits and develop our ability to respond in more novel and appropriate ways to new challenges. We can start to respond more mindfully to the demands in our environment.

Exercise

Flexibility

Think about your regular routine and how you spend the work day. Do you follow a very regular schedule? Why not change something this week about your work routine.

For example, vary the time you have lunch or the type of food you choose. Or why not do something different over your lunch period or have a morning break at a different time.

Now reflect on whether you enjoyed varying your routine. Did you feel in any way refreshed? Did you avoid any unhelpful habitual behaviours?

Emotional intelligence: Impulse control

Stein and Book (2006: 204) defined impulse control as 'the ability to delay an impulse, drive or temptation'. It's important not to confuse impulse control with a lack of spontaneity. People with impulse control problems are liable to lose their temper or act unpredictably and make highly risky choices without thinking through the consequences. They are not able to deal calmly with interruptions or frustrations. If you are able to show good impulse control it does not mean that you are out of touch with your instincts or feelings. It simply means that you are able to take the time to evaluate your options for responding to stimuli and make sensible choices before you commit to speech or action.

People with poor impulse control will often respond to a perceived criticism or attack by another person by losing their temper or lashing out. If you have a long-term or ongoing problem with impulse control you may find that that over time this causes damage to your personal and work relationships. You may end up being forced to leave jobs or experience multiple divorces or financial problems through reckless spending. If you recognise this as being a major problem then I would recommend therapy to discuss why impulse control is a problem for you.

It is possible that even if you do not have major problems with impulse control that you have some areas in your life where you can face conflict with others in response to particular triggers. A common situation where this happens can be emails. If we receive an email which we perceive as aggressive or confrontational from another person we can respond to this quickly by firing off an equally or even greater provocative email which can end up in a spiral of recrimination. We may later find that we have misread the email or jumped to conclusions. Even if the email was in fact impolite, firing off counter-attacks is not going to improve the situation. In those circumstances having a plan for dealing with this type of situation will help you to cope better. For example, you could resolve never to work on emails when you are feeling overly tired or frustrated. You could also decide that if you are annoyed by an email then you should wait for a defined period (e.g. 24 hours) before replying to it. You could also decide that if you have any negative feedback to give someone that this is done in a planned way in person rather than by email or phone.

If you are normally someone who responds thoughtfully and carefully to others but have recently become easily frustrated, impulsive or argumentative this could be a sign that you are experiencing a high degree of stress or even burnout. In this case you should take time to discuss your behaviour and feelings about it with someone you trust. If you conclude from this that you are experiencing problems with stress then you should seek help and support for this and find some way to get respite from your burdens.

Exercise

Impulse Control

Think about a situation in which you acted impulsively. Ask yourself how much thought, if any, went into your response. Then think about whether this is part of a pattern of impulsive behaviour or not. If you do have a tendency to react spontaneously in a negative way in certain situations then think about what these situations have in common. What are the triggers? What psychological function do you think your impulsive responses could be fulfilling? For example, do situations which trigger you activate any longstanding anxieties or threats to your self-esteem or represent any past conflicts or tap into painful memories?

What alternative strategy could you have for dealing with these situations? Now try to visualise yourself responding differently to that situation. At the earliest opportunity put your new behavioural response into practice.

Give yourself praise for having handled the situation differently. Focus on why you feel more satisfied with your improved response. Think about how you can embed your better response into your habitual way of responding to similar situations. One way of improving impulse control can be to write a flash card with instructions for how to deal with situations which you have problems with. You can have a list of things to do; for example, if your impulse problem was in dealing with emails as discussed above then you could have a card which says: 'If I receive an email which makes me angry then wait 24 hours before responding, ignore any content that is unimportant and find an alternative medium for dealing with any difficult issues.' If you then find yourself in the situation you can bring the card out of your purse or wallet as a reminder from your calm reasoning self about what to do.

Impulse control has important long-term consequences for career success. Stein and Book (2006) cited a famous longitudinal study by Shoda et al. (1997) which found that children who were able to delay gratification at age 4 demonstrated better social skills, better coping strategies and better scores in SAT tests at age 16–18 than children who were poor at delaying gratification. The experimental test which they took at age 4 was simply that they were offered the choice between eating one marshmallow on the table in front of them or waiting for an adult to return from an errand at which point they would be able to get two marshmallows rather than the one. The researchers found that the ability to delay gratification to get a larger reward later rather than a small reward instantly was a better predictor of SAT scores than their IQ.

If impulse control remains a problem for you in your adult relationships or your workplace then it is still worth working on behavioural control now. Building a successful and resilient career involves perseverance, application and dedication over a long period. There are no short cuts. Building up your portfolio of skills will take time with many of the rewards only being realised much further down the line.

Emotional intelligence: Happiness

Stein and Book (2006: 217) define happiness as a combination of 'self-satisfaction, general contentment and the ability to enjoy life'.

According to a survey by the Office of National Statistics (2015) the happiest place in Britain is the Fermanagh and Omagh areas of Northern Ireland. In the same study Northern Ireland came out best on most measures of wellbeing. I can easily understand this. Over the last few years I have visited Northern Ireland every year in my role as an external examiner. I feel great from the moment I land in the airport. Everyone I encounter is so courteous and genuine in their expression of friendship. People appear to take joy in small everyday things and the fact that the country has experienced a great deal of disharmony and poverty does not seem to detract from this.

We may experience a rush of exhilaration when we have a major achievement such as getting a new job that we wanted, buying a new home or finding out that we have passed a difficult exam. However, the joy of major achievements can often be short lived. To experience happiness more regularly and fully we need to be able to get enjoyment from small everyday things and be able to absorb ourselves completely when we are doing something which we really enjoy.

Positive psychology is a division of the psychology discipline which has tried to take on the issue of how we can enrich our lives and make ourselves happier and more contented. One writer from this field Mihali Csikszentmihályi (1990) has described the phenomenon of 'flow' as being a psychological state in which we are completely engaged in an enjoyable activity to the exclusion of everything else. A flow experience could be anything: painting a picture; an intense game of football with friends; sailing on a calm sea and enjoying the feel of sunshine on your skin; playing with your child. What distinguishes it as flow experience is a feeling of joy and total engagement. Csikszentmihályi suggested that we can improve our psychological outlook by trying to have as many flow experiences as we can. I am having a flow experience writing this book. Hopefully it shows and you are enjoying the experience of reading it. If you really enjoy your work and it continues to fulfil you then you should be able to experience flow at work. The reality of the demands of social work are such that this is not going to be possible all the time but hopefully you should have some good experiences in your social work career in which you help people to move their lives forward. Experiencing and recognising these feelings are important in maintaining the energy and enthusiasm which we need to go forward positively in our career and maintain a commitment and focus through periods of stress and strain.

Managers have a role in making the workplace more conducive to workers having flow experiences at work. Csikszentmihályi (2003) wrote 'The challenge for someone who wants to create an environment that attracts and retains enthusiastic and enterprising workers is to understand why people want to work in the first place, and then provide conditions that fulfill that need.' Social work is a profession which attracts people who want to help and support people to fulfil their potential. If management can keep this perspective in mind then it should be possible to create a workplace environment which facilitates staff in working towards this objective. Csikszentmihályi argued that a work environment which allows people to grow and develop will improve achievement and happiness of workers. An encouraging and nurturing environment will improve outcomes greatly for workers and ultimately the users of services as a result of the positive engagement of staff.

Exercise

Flow

Plan some time over the next week to do something which you really enjoy – perhaps a hobby or activity which you have not had enough time for recently. Stick to your plan and enjoy your relaxation time. Afterwards think about the degree to which you were able to tune out the background chatter of things which have been concerning you. Did you benefit from getting time and psychological space away from your everyday concerns? Close your eyes and imagine yourself experiencing the activity again. Reflect on whether you allow yourself enough time for relaxing activities that allow you to unwind completely. Think about how you could manage your time better to allow you to set aside more time for complete relaxation.

Emotional intelligence: Optimism

Stein and Book (2006: 230) described optimism as 'the ability to look at the brighter side of life and maintain a positive attitude even in the face of adversity'. They stated that optimism does not mean seeing everything in life through rose-tinted spectacles but is rather an ability to be realistic while retaining a conviction that we can learn from mistakes, work towards positive goals and take advantage of opportunities when they arise. In Chapter 2, I described Burns's list of common cognitive errors such as 'all or nothing thinking' and over-generalisation, which can lead us to a pattern of self-defeating thought processes. A person with optimism is able to see which part of the reason for their failures is in external circumstances and does not take temporary setbacks as personally as someone with a pessimistic thinking style. They are able to resolve to try better next time and plan how they are going to tackle the situation differently rather than working on the assumption that they will always fail.

Exercise

Optimism

Think about a setback which you recently had either in your personal or professional life. Think about why it upset you. What thoughts went through your mind about the implications of what happened? Did you think that the incident was isolated to the particular situation or related to some more global failing on your part? Did you take the view that you could overcome the problem and achieve a better outcome in the future? Think about the relation between your thoughts about the situation and what your feelings were.

If you had been left with negative thoughts about yourself or depressed feelings about your abilities or personal qualities then try to reframe how you think about the situation. Think about what qualities you have which might help you to handle a similar situation differently in the future. If there is a need for you to acquire additional knowledge or additional skills then think about what you might have to do to acquire these things. Put together a plan of how you can become better prepared to deal with a similar situation in the future. Now think about how it makes you feel now that you have a plan for dealing with your difficult task or situation. Do you feel any more confident or positive?

Dealing with negative thoughts and feelings: Emotional agility

David and Congleton (2013) stated that there can be two habitual responses which people can have for dealing with negative thoughts and feelings – both of which are self-defeating in the long run. One is to suppress them, only for them to re-occur as themes again in other situations over long periods of time. Another response can be to give in to the negative impulse by, for example, becoming angry with another person or giving into depressed feelings about ourselves. David and Congleton suggest an approach which borrows from cognitive psychology. That is that we should clearly label in our minds what the negative thoughts are which we are having and acknowledge that they are thoughts and that they belong to us. We should then identify what emotions have arisen in us as a result of these thoughts. Again, we should identify clearly for ourselves that they are feelings and that we own them.

David and Congleton stated that this action of identifying and labelling thoughts and feelings allows you to see that they are information about your current state of mind and that they may change over time. You can accept that you are having these thoughts and feelings without having to respond to them right away. Having clearly identified the thoughts and feelings which we have about a difficult situation, we can then give ourselves space to decide on a response which is consistent with our values.

Developing emotional agility over time will help us to become more in tune with who we are, what we really feel and respond to difficult situations in ways which are most helpful to us in the long term.

Exercise

Emotional Agility

The next time you feel brought down by a setback or feel you have responded to a difficult situation in a way which you are unhappy with, work through the following questions.

1. What were the different stages in the incident or conversation? What was it about my reaction which left me feeling unhappy?
2. What were the thoughts which went through my head?
3. What feelings arose from the thoughts?
4. Did I respond in a careful considered way, did I respond on an impulse without thinking, or did I respond by denying my feelings and trying to ignore my thoughts and feelings?
5. Does the incident remind me of previous situations in which I have had similar difficulties?
6. What values and qualities would I like to be able to show if I were faced with a similar situation again?
7. How could I respond in the future in a way which was more congruent with the values I identified above?

Developing creative thinking skills

In Chapter 8 I introduced the concept of professional curiosity and why it was important in enabling social workers to identify and face up to new issues and professional challenges. Thinking creatively is also important for managing our career and thinking about how one can develop professionally.

Social work is constantly facing new challenges as a result of societal change. Female genital mutilation, honour-based violence and radicalisation, for example, are problems which are widely discussed in social work media now, but were little understood only a few years ago. Even now, the profession is in the early stages of thinking about how we can tackle these problems. Finding approaches to these emerging problems requires imagination and creativity.

Kelley and Kelley (2012) stated that as children we are extremely creative because we are not self-conscious about drawing or writing or thinking unusual things. However, when we get into our teens formal education tends to set up a dividing line between people who are creative and those who are not. For example, I used to love drawing when I was in primary school. However, when I went to secondary school my art teacher told me that I had some talent but not enough to make a career out of art – so that was that – I went down a purely academic route. Kelley and Kelley say that we need to reawaken our child-like sensibilities to rediscover our creative side. We can do this by getting outside of our office, our procedures and our comfort zone. They suggest that we should try to stop our internal 'judge' from interfering and allow ourselves space to uncritically think about ideas and come up with new solutions to problems. For example, is there scope for taking a community or group work approach with some of the problems you are dealing with on your patch? Kelley and Kelley (p. 118) have a mantra, 'Don't get ready, get started.' They suggest that taking small steps towards a goal is the best way to overcome nerves about trying something innovative or creative in our work. Thus, if we want to try to tackle emerging social problems the first stage has to be making a start in engaging with people in local communities who have knowledge of these problems.

Managing career changes successfully

The profession is currently facing a great deal of structural change partly as a response to government spending restrictions and partly as result of local authorities moving from being direct employers to commissioning services from independent providers. I discussed the issue of social work practices in Chapter 5 and looked at potential positives and negatives of these changes for social workers. Originally, it was only services such as home care and residential care which were privatised. However, some local authorities are currently thinking about outsourcing assessment and fieldwork services. It is likely that this trend will continue. Making a change from working in a local authority to working as part of some sort of social work practice or community interest company involves fundamental changes in both your security of employment and the amount of control which you have over your work and your career. There are new risks and uncertainties, new challenges and new freedoms and opportunities. It represents complex change.

Brimm (2015) suggested a framework for dealing with complex change in the world of work based around seven Cs: Complexity, Clarity, Confidence, Creativity, Commitment, Consolidation and Change. I will describe the seven Cs and how they might be applied to dealing with organisational change in social work.

The first C, complexity, involves thinking carefully through all the issues that apply to your situation. It may be the changes have been initiated externally – e.g. that the local authority which you work for has decided to restructure – or internally – e.g. that you have independently decided that you want to work for yourself. Regardless of where the change has been instigated you will have choices. If your employer restructures then the choices will be about whether to leave or to stay. Thinking through this will involve gathering information about how your job will change if you stay and also what alternative positions might be available with other employers. If you are considering working for yourself this involves detailed consideration of the costs, benefits and risks of such a decision and talking this through with your family. Decisions such as this are detailed and there are likely to be many interrelated issues, such as where you will live, whether you can afford to take on a mortgage, etc.

The second C is about seeking clarity. Once you have identified all the implications of the options in a complex decision the next stage is to think about their relative importance and get a clear idea of how important they are to you. For example, if you are just about to start a family then it may not be the best time financially to think about working for yourself. Alternatively, if your partner has a stable income then the flexibility of working from home may tip the balance towards working for yourself at this time. By taking time to think deeply about what is important to you personally and professionally you can increase the chance of the decision you make being one that is right for you.

The third C is confidence. Brimm stated that there is an optimal amount of confidence which will empower us to deal with change competently and decisively while avoiding being reckless or rash and failing to think through important issues. If we are feeling anxious about a new role then getting a mentor who has managed the same transition effectively can be a way of getting support.

The fourth C is creativity and this involves freeing ourselves up creatively to come up with new strategies for dealing with our new responsibilities or the new structure we find ourselves in. As I stated in the section above this means freeing oneself intellectually. A holiday or a break of some sort before starting a new role can be helpful in giving yourself the ability to change.

The fifth C is commitment. The Roman god Janus was the god of transitions and gateways. He had two faces, one looking forward and one looking back. When we are at a career transition we too will be at a boundary where we will looking back at our recent work and experiences, possibly with some sadness and loss and also looking forward, perhaps with a mixture of excitement and trepidation. To make our transition successful we need to implement the fifth C by making a wholehearted commitment to our new path in spite of our regrets about leaving the old one and our anxieties about what lies ahead.

The sixth C is consolidation. The task now is to begin to find your identity in your new role or organisation. This can be a difficult phase as it involves adapting to new ways of working and embedding new skills and new perspectives. Enjoying the company of friends and doing leisure activities which you enjoy are good ways of maintaining continuity in at least some parts of your life while you adjust to a new role.

The final C is change and this involves dealing with all the new challenges which will come with your new job role. Even after you have adapted to a new role, change will continue to come and you may eventually find yourself contemplating how to deal with a whole new set of changes.

Dealing with setbacks and disappointments

Even if we approach our career building with optimism and confidence we will inevitably have failures and disappointments. There will be the promotion which we missed or the career move which did not live up to what we hoped it would be. It is easy in these situations to start to feel anger and resentment and these emotions can build up to the extent that they can overtake us and consume us. We have probably all experienced a situation where we have a friend who is frustrated about some sort of injustice at work and who talks incessantly about it every time we see them. We may have had issues like this ourselves sometimes but not realise it because friends are too polite to point out how obsessively we have been focused on it. In these situations the self-talk and negative emotions are going to be damaging to us psychologically and physically. The Dalai Lama (Dalai Lama and Cutler, 2003) suggested that we should carry out deep reflection into our thoughts and feelings and consider whether our emotions might be damaging to us. He suggested that we should reflect on previous times in our life when we let ourselves be overtaken by such emotions and consider what effect it had on our relationships with others and our ability to live life positively. If we can put negative feelings aside then we can start to put together a credible plan to improve our situation. This may well involve looking for another job. However, if we can find greater contentment in the short term then this will make us stronger and better able to recognise and take advantage of opportunities when they come along.

Holiday (2014) said that if we are unable to accept setbacks and take the view that life is against us then this is akin to taking a red traffic light as a personal attack. He suggested that we reflect on how much worse the setback could have been. We should accept that the course of our life will have unpleasant blips in it. In the longer term we can triumph against career setbacks and in fact they may send us in a different direction which is ultimately more fulfilling. In any case, falling prey to defeatism or anger is not going to help us to improve our situation.

Intelligent CV creation

A curriculum vitae (or resume) is not just a record of achievement, it is a valuable tool which can help you to think creatively about your skills and experience and widen the range of jobs you might consider applying for.

I would recommend that as soon as you graduate as a social worker you put together a CV. You may think that this is unnecessary as most UK social work jobs ask for an application form to be completed rather than a CV. However, writing a CV and constantly updating it has several advantages. First of all, you will have a comprehensive and regularly updated list of all your qualifications, training, achievements and previous responsibilities all in one easily accessible place. Thus, for example, when you are filling in an application form you are not struggling to remember exactly which year you got your Practice Education qualification or the exact title of that residential work job you did just before your social work degree. Second, it helps to remind you of exactly how experienced and well qualified you are. Writing a CV can be a real confidence booster. Why would anybody **not** want to employ you with such an impressive list of training, education and experience?

I would recommend having a comprehensive CV which lists everything. Then, if you are asked to submit a CV for a specific job you can produce an edited version for that particular job which highlights some aspects of your career and qualifications and omits small pieces of training or experience which are not relevant. It is absolutely essential that everything in your CV and any job application is truthful. This does not mean that you have to be modest. You should certainly talk up what you have done but you must still be honest. I once saw an article on the *Guardian* website in which the journalist suggested that everyone lied in job applications. Perhaps this is the case in certain parts of the media but it is an absolute no no in jobs in health and social care where trust is of paramount importance. If you are talking about work in which you have been part of a project team, you should clarify what your role was in the work rather than just saying you were involved in the work.

You can find templates for CVs easily on the internet. Pick one that is clear and straightforward. My CV has the following headings: Profile, Experience, Education and Training, Papers and Publications. The first heading 'Profile' is something which is worth doing, but I would recommend that you do this section last. The Profile is a brief description of yourself which would make you attractive to an employer. It should sum up what sort of work you are capable of, your most important qualifications, your professional identity and something about your attitude to work. For example, 'I am a committed child protection social worker with 5 years' frontline experience. I am a qualified practice educator and have undertaken training in family therapy. I am an enthusiastic team member and have considerable experience in joint work with the Police and other agencies and professionals.'

In the section on Experience you should list all your posts in order, starting with the current or most recent one and working back. For each post you should list the name of the employer, the job title, a list of your responsibilities and also a list of what you consider to be your achievements in the post. Achievements can be any special contributions you made, such as a very complex case or group of cases which you were involved with or a piece of group work or project work which you undertook or perhaps a forum or study group which you set up. It is important to record these achievements because when you go for job interviews, employers will want to know of instances where you showed initiative, innovation or took responsibility.

The section on Education and Training should list every piece of training and education you have had from short in-house courses on the Care Act to degree qualifications. Of course, when you come to completing a job application form or are sending the CV to an employer you may want to miss out very short courses which are not relevant to the job being applied for. Application forms normally have separate sections for education and training and it is not always clear which of these categories some courses fall into. When I am in doubt I try to think about what is going to make sense to the person reading the form and have regard to the amount of space available in each section. I tend to miss out or just summarise my school qualifications as they were a very long time ago and not very salient any more for the type of jobs I am applying for. However, that will probably not be the case for all readers.

The last section on Papers and Publications is a relevant section for me because I am an academic. Some readers may want to include this section to highlight any research or publication you have been involved with. Alternatively, you might want to have a section which highlights special projects or large pieces of work you have been involved with.

I don't have a section in my CV for hobbies or interests. I don't honestly think most people are interested in this and it can just lead to people making assumptions about you based on their prejudices or preconceptions. If you are asked for hobbies and interests on an application form I would tend to list interests which you have that are either neutral or likely to be regarded positively.

Exercise

CV Creation

Now I would like you to create a CV for yourself that sets out who you are and what knowledge and skills you have to offer. If you do this well, it will be a useful skeleton on to which you can add all the new skills and experiences which you gain as you progress as a social worker. It will also provide you with a record which you can use to evidence your professional development if required to do so by the professional regulator.

After you have completed your CV, reflect on how you feel about having listed all your experience and accomplishments. Hopefully it will have given you a confidence boost.

Your CV is the real source of your job security and employability

My mother had a very strong view when I was growing up that public service was the key to job security. She thought that I ought to join the civil service and that doing this would guarantee me a career structure, a good pension and a job for life. I was a big disappointment to her when I quit my job with the Audit Commission to do voluntary work. I never looked back of course, and forged an alternative career structure which nobody but me seems to be capable of understanding.

There is no prescription for career success that someone else can give you. You will have to find your own path. However, I am firmly of the view that employability and job security are qualities which reside in the individual worker and not in their employer or any contract they have with them. We are living in a time in which globalisation, information technology and outsourcing are radically and rapidly changing the nature and structure of human services work. For example, if we are employed by a local authority we cannot be certain that it is going to continue to be our employer in the future. We cannot be sure either that our job role will continue to exist or that it will continue to be done by people with the same experience or job title that we have. A permanent post can turn out to be extremely impermanent as a result of austerity policies and privatisation. This is not just a feature of the public sector. Many professional roles in the private sector are being outsourced too so that employers can exploit specialist skills for short-term pieces of work. Levinson (2015) described this as a 'new age of self-reliance' in which employers no longer expect to have long-term relationships with their employees. He said that workers need to keep in mind alternative roles which they look to if their current employment comes to an end. Levinson stated that specialist skills can lose their currency and marketability. He suggests that workers should think about their fundamental personal qualities and generic skills and how these can be transferred from one work environment to another. For example, an ability to use a particular computer package is something which is of little use if that package becomes obsolete. However, an interest in information technology and an ability to adapt quickly and enthusiastically to new forms of IT is a very useful quality. Similarly, the skills of networking, teamworking or leadership which we develop as a social worker can be easily adapted to new work settings.

Marc Andreessen (2007), a venture capitalist, said it is impossible to plan a career in the rapidly changing environment which we are in today. He stated, 'Instead of planning your career, focus on developing skills and pursuing opportunities.' He suggested that just as a professional investor spreads their risk by having a portfolio of investments so the professional should look on their career as a portfolio of jobs, roles and opportunities. My own career has involved working as a social worker, a team manager, a project manager, a lecturer and a head of a department. Each successive job has been an opportunity to enhance and widen my portfolio of skills and experience. I have on occasion taken a reduction in terms and conditions or salary to get a job which will improve my marketability in the longer term. Sometimes, counter-intuitively, there may be greater advantage in taking a temporary job if it allows you to gain access to a field which is difficult to break into, or gives you experience which you think could be in demand in the future. Clearly, your personal circumstances will influence your appetite for risk, but a permanent post is not always the low risk option it once was. If you do have a permanent job you should be taking advantage of the relative stability to improve your skills portfolio. Speaking on the James Altucher podcast (Altucher, 2015), business writer Taylor Pearson stated that workers can be earning a regular salary but at the same time accumulating a 'silent risk' by not developing skills which can be applied to a wider job marketplace if their current job disappears.

Of course, there are collective as well as individual ways of influencing the future direction of your profession, and hence your career options. You could join the British Association of Social Workers (BASW) or the Social Work Action Network (SWAN). Both of these organisations are standing up for the profession, raising awareness about issues and helping social workers to stand together for their voice to be heard. SWAN additionally promotes links with social work in other countries to provide an international perspective and allow social workers to make connections across the world.

New technology

I remember in the early 1990s a friend of my wife and I went on a professional exchange visit to Japan. She gave a talk to a group of Japanese social care professionals about social care in Britain. At the end she opened the floor to questions. She told us that the first question that someone asked her was, 'What progress have you made in the UK with robots?' Our friend did not know what to make of this question and when she told us about it, my wife and I fell about laughing. We thought the idea was ridiculous. It was not a concept that seemed alien to the Japanese, however. The Japanese animator Katsuhiro Otomo had made an anime film in 1991 called *Roujin Z*, which was a futuristic parody about a robotic suit which could give personal care to an older person.

Now fast forward almost two decades to 2010. At this time I was working as a project manager, responsible for a range of social care projects which used new technologies such as satellite tracking for people with dementia. I found myself on a steering group of a project which was going to design social care robots, alongside robotocists and engineers. What had once seemed like science fiction was coming closer to reality.

Technology is moving faster than ever. It has great potential to enhance social care and social work. Maintaining an interest in emerging and developing technology is an important way of future proofing your career. If you can combine a good skill set as a social worker with an interest and understanding of technology then you will be well placed to take advantage of job opportunities which will undoubtedly develop around technology. Nourbakhsh (2015) stated that over the next two decades medical robotics will make wheelchairs obsolete and visually impaired people will be aided by cameras and sensors. Nourbakhsh stated that these innovations could be an early step towards transhumanism, a future state in which highly sophisticated hybrids of humans and machines (cyborgs) will be able to out-perform purely biological humans. Such possibilities will have many associated ethical dilemmas and will challenge our understanding of what it is to be human.

Exercise

Managing the Future

In this chapter I have looked at the issues around rapidly changing technological and economic factors and the importance of maintaining a broad and up-to-date range of professional skills. Now I want you to think about how you can help to shape your future. You will all be familiar with the concept of forecasting. That is, looking at current

(Continued)

(Continued)

trends and extrapolating from them to make predictions about phenomena such as the weather and the future state of the economy. Robinson (1990) invented the concept of 'backcasting'. This involves deciding on a future state of affairs which we find desirable and then working backwards in time to consider what policies and initiatives would be necessary to bring about this state of affairs.

The exercise which I would like you to do contains elements of forecasting and backcasting. I would like you to consider the following questions:

1.   How do you think your profession will have changed five years from now? Now think about how the field you work in may have changed 10 years from now. Think about current trends in the law, politics, social policy and employment practices and the possible influences of developing technologies. How do you think all these influences will affect the types of job opportunities which will be available in your field or area of interest?
2.   Now think about how you would like to fit into the job marketplace of the future. Do you want to be a manager, a practitioner, an agency worker, a consultant...?
3.   Think about what sorts of skills and experience will be needed to meet the opportunities that will be available.
4.   Make a plan for how you are going to obtain the necessary experience and skills over the next few years to improve your career options over the next decade.

Of course, none of us have the ability to genuinely predict the future with any degree of certainty. However, we can resolve to actively manage our skill set and our career. In so doing we can be like an able navigator and have the winds and the waves on our side. We will have a career which is resilient and fulfilling for us and socially useful for the society we live in.

Chapter recap

In this final chapter I returned to the concept of mindfulness and asked you to think about how it could help you to think objectively about your work and your career and whether you are progressing towards medium- and long-term goals. I then moved on to look at some of the components of emotional intelligence which can be helpful in building resilience into your career in the long term.

The second half of the chapter looked at the changing nature of work and careers in the twenty-first century in response to factors such as globalisation and technological change. I set out the view that your career success and your long-term job security are grounded in your portfolio of skills and experience rather than in any one job role or employer. The chapter finished with an exercise in thinking about where you want to be in your career in the future and how you might get there.

Further reading

The *Community Care* website is an essential resource for anyone working in social work or social care and I would recommend that you sign up for daily emails which carry the latest social care headlines and links to the articles. The *Guardian* newspaper site also has social care pages and you can sign up for news alerts with them also. Keeping up to date with what is happening in your profession is essential.

If you want to keep in touch with technological changes in society then an excellent resource is *Wired* magazine which is available in US and UK editions. They also, of course, have a website.

I would also recommend reading as widely as you can. If you use Twitter then you can follow feeds from organisations such as the HCPC, BASW, SWAN and Department of Health. Try to read a newspaper regularly, either a paper copy or online and vary which paper you read so that you get exposed to a range of ideas and perspectives.

Final note

I hope you have enjoyed this book and that it is helpful to you in developing a resilient and fulfilling career in which you achieve positive changes for the people you work with. I would love to hear your experiences of reading and using the book. Please follow the Twitter account for this book @ResilientSW. You can also message me through this account. Please also consider leaving a review on Amazon. Academic books don't often get reviewed, but by taking a few minutes to share your thoughts you can help other readers decide whether this book is going to helpful to them.

REFERENCES

Achor, S. (2012) 'Positive intelligence', *Harvard Business Review*, January–February 2012.

Adam Smith Institute/Unison (2014) *Outsourcing the Cuts: Payment and employment effects of contracting out*. Available at: http://smithinstitutethinktank.files.wordpress.com/2014/09/outsourcing-the-cuts-pay-and-employment-effects-of-contracting-out.pdf

Allen, D. (2001) *Getting Things Done: How to achieve stress-free productivity*. London: Piatkus.

Altucher, J. (2014) 'Ask Altucher' Episode 101. To Do Lists Are a Waste of Time. Podcast. http://m.youtube.com/watch?v=Q-9MLqEvGDsf

Altucher, J. (2015) James Altucher Podcast Episode 309. www.sticher.com/podcast/stansberry-radio-network/askaltucher/e/ep/-309-the-end-of-jobs-39657624

Altucher, J. and Altucher, C.A. (2014) *The Power of No*. Carlsbad, CA: Hay House Inc.

Amabile, T.M. and Khaire, M. (2008) 'Creativity and the role of the leader', *Harvard Business Review*, October 2008.

Andreessen, M. (2007) PMARCA Guide to Career Planning part 1. Available at: http://pmarchive.com/guide_to_career_planning_part1.html

Banks, S. (2012) *Ethics and Values in Social Work*. London: Palgrave Macmillan/BASW.

Baron, R.A. and Byrne, D. *Social Psychology* (10th edition). Boston: Allyn and Bacon.

Bass, B.M. and Riggio, R.E. (2006) *Transformational Leadership* (2nd edition). Mahwah, NJ: Lawrence Erlbaum.

Bee, M. (2015) 'Social work is the perfect profession to embrace hot desking'. *Community Care*, 2 July 2015. Available at: http://www.communitycare.co.uk/2015/07/02/whats-wrong-hot-desking/?cmpid=NLC|SCSC|SCDDB-2015-0703

Beck, A.T., Rush, A.J., Shaw, B.F. and Emery, G. (1979) *Cognitive Therapy of Depression*. New York: Guilford Press.

Benight, C.C. and Bandura, A. (2004) 'Social cognitive theory of post-traumatic recovery: The role of perceived self-efficacy', *Behavior Research and Therapy*, 42: 1129–48.

Benight, C.C. and Cieslak, R. (2011) 'Cognitive factors and resilience: how self-efficacy contributes to coping with adversities', in S.M. Southwick, B.T. Litz, D. Charney and M.J. Friedman (eds), *Resilience and Mental Health: Challenges across the lifespan*. New York: Cambridge University Press.

Black, J. and Miller, D. (2008) *The Toyota Way to Healthcare Excellence: Increase efficiency and improve quality with Lean*. Chicago, IL: Health Administration Press.

Block, J.H. and Turula, E. (1963) 'Identification, ego control and adjustment', *Child Development*, 34, 945–53.

Boldt, L.G. (1993) *Zen and the Art of Making a Living*. New York: Penguin Books USA.

Bonanno, G.A. (2004) 'Loss, trauma and human resilience: Have we underestimated the human capacity to thrive after extremely aversive events?', *American Psychologist*, 59: 20–8.

Breaking Bad. TV series. Episode 5.16 'Felina'. AMC.

Brimm, L. (2015) 'How to embrace complex change', *Harvard Business Review*, September 2015.

British Association of Social Workers (BASW) (2012a) *The State of Social Work 2012*. Available at: http://cdn.basw.co.uk/upload/basw_23651-3.pdf

British Association of Social Workers (BASW) (2012b) *BASW Social Media Policy*. Available at: http://cdn.basw.co.uk/upload/basw_34634-1.pdf

British Association of Social Workers (BASW) (2012c) *The Professional Capabilities Framework*. Available at: http://www.basw.co.uk/pcf

Brown, D. (2011) *The Experiments: The secret of luck*. TV programme. Available at: http://www.channel4.com/programmes/derren-brown-the-experiments/episode-guide

Brown, G.W. and Harris, T. (1978) *Social Origins of Depression: Study of psychiatric disorder in women*. London: Tavistock.

Bugg-Levine, A., Kogut, B. and Kulatilaka, N. (2012) 'A new approach to funding social enterprises', *Harvard Business Review*, January–February 2012.

Burka, J.B. and Yuen L.B. (2008) *Procrastination: Why you do it, what to do about it now*. Cambridge, MA: Da Capo Lifelong Books.

Burns, D.D. (2008) *Feeling Good: The new mood therapy*. New York: Avon Books.

Burns. J.M. (2012) *Leadership*. New York: Open Road Integrated Media.

Burns, R. (1786) *To a Louse* (poem).

Carlyle, T. (1849) *Heroes, Hero Worship and the Heroic in History*. Boston, MA: Houghton-Mifflin.

Carnegie, D. (2006) *How to Win Friends and Influence People*. London: Random House.

Carroll, M. (2009) 'At times of risk and stress, cultivate stillness', in Barry Boyce (ed.), *In the Face of Fear: Buddhist wisdom for challenging times*. Boston, MA: Shambhala Publications.

Casey, L.C.B. (2015) *Report of Inspection of Rotherham Borough Council*. London: Department for Communities and Local Government. Available at: https://www.gov.uk/government/uploads/system/uploads/attachment_data/file/401125/46966_Report_of_Inspection_of_Rotherham_WEB.pdf

Castillo, Richard (1997) *Culture & Mental Illness: A client-centered approach*. Pacific Grove, CA: Brooks/Cole Publishing Company.

Cherniss, C. (1980a) *Professional Burnout in Human Service Organizations*. New York: Praeger.

Cherniss, C. (1980b) *Staff Burnout: Job Stress in the Human Services*. Sage Studies in Community Mental Health. Beverley Hills, CA: Sage.

Community Care (2009) Exclusive Survey: Media Coverage of Social Work is Mostly Negative. Available at: http://www.communitycare.co.uk/2009/05/12/exclusive-survey-media-coverage-of-social-work-is-mostly-negative/

CNN (2011) Defiant Japanese Boat Captain Rode Out Tsunami. Available at: http://edition.cnn.com/2011/WORLD/asiapcf/04/03/japan.tsunami.captain/

Crawford, N. (1992) 'The psychology of the bully', in Andrea Adams (ed.), *Bullying at Work*. London: Virago.

Cree, V.E., Claptoin, G. and Smith, M. (2015) Series Editors' Preface, in V. E Cree (ed.), *The State*. Bristol: Policy Press.

Cryer, B., McCraty, R. and Childre, D. (2003) 'Pull the plug on stress', *Harvard Business Review*, July 2003.

Csikszentmihályi, M. (1990) *Flow: The psychology of optimal experience*. London: Rider (Random House).

Csikszentmihályi, M. (2003) *Good Business: Leadership, flow and the making of meaning*. New York: Viking/Penguin.

Dailey, D.M. (1983) 'Androgyny, sex role stereotypes and clinical judgement', *Social Work Research and Abstracts*, 19 (1): 20–4.

Dalai Lama and Cutler, H.C. (2003) *The Art of Happiness at Work*. London: Hodder and Stoughton.

David, S. and Congelton, C. (2013) 'Emotional agility', *Harvard Business Review*, November 2013.

Department for Education (2012) *Social Work Practices: Report of the national evaluation*. Available at: https://www.gov.uk/government/publications/social-work-practices-report-of-the-national-evaluation

Department for Education (2015) *Knowledge and Skills Statements for Practice Leaders and Practice Supervisors*. Available at: www.gov.uk/government/publications/knowledge-and-skills-statements-for-child-and-family-social-work

Dewey, J. (1933) *How We Think*. Boston, MA: DC Health.

Dewey, J. (1938) *Logic: The theory of inquiry*. Troy, MN: Reinhart and Winston.

Egan, G. (2013) *The Skilled Helper* (10th edition). Belmont, CA: Brooks/Cole.

Faber, M.A. and Mayer, J.D. (2009) 'Resonance to archetypes in media: There's some accounting for taste', *Journal of Research in Personality*, 43: 307–22.

Farber, B.A. (1983) 'Introduction: A critical perspective on burnout', in B.A. Farber (ed.), *Stress and Burnout in the Human Service Professions*. Oxford: Elsevier.

Fayard, A-L. and Weeks, J. (2011) 'Who moved my cube?' *Harvard Business Review*, July–August 2011.

Feder, A., Charney, D. and Collins, K. (2011) 'Neurobiology of resilience', in S.M. Southwick, B.T. Litz, D. Charney and M.J. Friedman (eds), *Resilience and Mental Health: Challenges across the lifespan*. New York: Cambridge University Press.

Feder, A., Nestler, E.J., Westphal, M. and Charney, D.S. (2010) 'Psychobiological mechanisms of resilience to stress', in J.W. Reich, A.J. Zautra and J.S. Hall (eds), *Handbook of Adult Resilience*. New York: Guilford Press.

Ferguson, I. (2008) *Reclaiming Social Work: Challenging neoliberalism and promoting social justice*. London: Sage.

Field, A. (2003) 'Don't let stress strain communication' Harvard Business Management Letter. January 2003.

Financial Times, 31 May 2011, 'The shameful state of UK care homes'. Available at: http://www.ft.com/cms/s/0/7d550be4-8bb6-11e0-a725-00144feab49a.html#axzz3hUG4JWdk

Fiore, N. (2007) *The Now Habit*. Revised edition. New York: Tarcher/Penguin.

Fook, J. (2002) *Social Work Critical Theory and Practice*. London: Sage.

Fowler, D., Garety, P. and Kuipers, E. (1995) *Cognitive Therapy for Psychosis: Theory and practice*. Chichester: John Wiley and Sons.

Freeman, D., Garety, P.A., Bebbington, P., Slater, M., Kuipers, E., Fowler, D., et al. (2005) 'The psychology of persecutory ideation II: A virtual reality experimental study', *Journal of Nervous and Mental Disease*, 193: 309–15.

Friedman, R. (2015) 'Regular exercise is part of your job', *Harvard Business Review On-Point*, Spring 2015.

Furedi, F. (2013) *Moral Crusades in an Age of Mistrust*. Basingstoke: Palgrave Macmillan.

Gergen, C. and Vanourek, G. (2015) 'Three ways to beat burnout', *Harvard Business Review On-Point*, Spring 2015.

Gibbon, E. (1776) *The History of the Decline and Fall of the Roman Empire*. London: Strahan and Cadell.

Greer, J. (2014) 'How social work can tackle its morale problem', *Guardian* Social Care Network. Available at: http://www.theguardian.com/social-care-network/social-life-blog/2014/sep/03/social-work-tackle-morale-problem

Gyatso, T. – HH Dalai Lama (1999) *Ancient Wisdom, Modern World*. London: Little, Brown and Company.

Harris, J. (2003) *The Social Work Business*. Abingdon: Routledge.

Harris, J. (2007) 'Looking backward, looking forward: Current trends in human service management', in J. Aldgate, L. Healy, B. Malcolm, B. Pine, W. Rose and J. Seden (eds), *Enhancing Social Work Management: Theory and best practice from the UK and USA*. London: Jessica Kingsley.

Hasson, G. (2015) *How to Deal with Difficult People: Smart tactics for overcoming problem people in your life*. Chichester: Capstone Publishing.

Hawkins, P. and Shohet, R. (2006) *Supervision in the Helping Professions* (3rd edition). Maidenhead: Open University Press/ McGraw Hill.

Healy, K. (2005) *Social Work Theories in Context: Creating frameworks for practice*. Basingstoke: Palgrave Macmillan.

Hesse, A.R. (2002) 'Secondary trauma: How working with trauma survivors affects therapists', *Clinical Social Work Journal*, 30 (3): 293–309.

Hochschild, A.R. (1983) *The Managed Heart: Commercialization of human feeling*. Berkeley, CA: University of California Press.

Hogg, M.A. and Vaughn, G.M. (2013) *Social Psychology* (7th edition). Harlow: Pearson.

Holiday, R. (2014) *The Obstacle is the Way*. London: Profile Books.

Jackson, T., Burgess, A. and Edwards, J. (2006). 'A simple approach to improving email communication: Going back to basics', *Communications of the ACM*, 49(6): 107–9. Accessed on 25/07/2015 at https://dspace.lboro.ac.uk/dspace-jspui/bitstream/2134/2191/3/jackson_simple_approach.pdf

Janis, I.L. (1972) *Victims of Groupthink: A psychological study of foreign policy decisions and fiascos*. Boston, MA: Houghton Mifflin.

Jones, R. (2015) 'Plans to privatise child protection are moving at pace', *Guardian* website, 12 January 2015. Available at: http://www.theguardian.com/social-care-network/2015/jan/12/child-protection-privatisation-ray-jones

Kadushin, A. and Harkness, D. (2002) *Supervision in Social Work* (4th edition). New York: Columbia University Press.

Kaufman, S.B. (2015) 'Your passion for work could ruin your career', *Harvard Business Review On-Point*, Spring 2015.

Kellaway, L. (2013) 'Must I check my emails on holiday?' *Financial Times*, 13 August 2013.

Kelley, T. and Kelley, D. (2012) 'Reclaim your creative confidence', *Harvard Business Review*, December 2012.

Knapton, S. (2014) '"Thatcher gene" is key to needing less sleep', *The Telegraph*, 1 August 2014.

Knott, C. and Scragg, T. (2010) *Reflective Practice in Social Work* (2nd edition). Exeter: Learning Matters.

Kobasa, S.C. (1979) 'Stressful life events, personality and health: an enquiry into hardiness', *Journal of Personality and Social Psychology*, 37: 1–11.

LaFontaine, J.S. (1994) *Extent and Nature of Ritual and Organised Abuse*. London: HMSO.

Landy, F.J. (2005) 'Some historical and scientific issues related to research on emotional intelligence', *Journal of Organizational Behavior*, 26: 411–24.

Lange, K. (2011) 'Writing habits of Ian Fleming'. Available at: www.kennethlange.com/writing_habits_of_ian_fleming.html. Accessed 19 July 2015.

Langer, E. (2014) 'Mindfulness in the age of complexity', *Harvard Business Review,* March 2014.

LaTorra, M. (1993) *A Warrior Blends with Life: A Modern Tao*. Berkeley, CA: North Atlantic Books.

Leider, R. and Buchholz, S. (1995) 'The Rustout Syndrome', *Training and Development*, 49 (3) March 1995.

Levinson, H. (2015) 'A new age of self reliance', *Harvard Business Review On-Point*, Spring 2015: 54.

Lewis, G. and Sloggett, A. (1998) 'Suicide, deprivation and unemployment', *British Medical Journal*, 7168: 1283–7.

Local Government Association (LGA) (2014a) *The Standards for Employers of Social Workers in England*. Available at: www.local.gov.uk/documents/10180/6188796/The_standards_for_employers_of_social_workers.pdf/fb7cb809-650c-4ccd-8aa7-fecb07271c4a

Local Government Association (LGA) (2014b) *Future Funding Outlook 2014: Funding outlook for councils to 2019/20*. Available at: www.local.gov.uk/documents/10180/5854661/L14-340+Future+funding+-+initial+draft.pdf/1854420d-1ce0-49c5-8515-062dccca2c70

Lindert, J., von Ehrenstein, O.S., Grashow, R., Gal, G., Braehler, E. and Weisskopf, M.G. (2014) 'Sexual and physical abuse in childhood is associated with depression and anxiety over the life course: Systematic review and meta-analysis', *Int J Public Health*, 59 (2): 359–72.

Locke, E.A. (2005) 'Why emotional intelligence is an invalid concept', *Journal of Organizational Behavior*, 26 (4): 425–31.

Lubit, R.H. (2004) *Coping with Toxic Managers, Subordinates and Other Difficult People*. Upper Saddle River, NJ: Financial Times Press.

Lynn, R. (2010) 'Mindfulness in social work education', *Social Work Education*, 29: 289–304.

Manthorpe, J., Moriarty, J., Hussein, S., Stevens, M. and Sharpe, E. (2015) 'Content and purpose of supervision in social work practice in England: Views of newly qualified social workers, managers and directors', *British Journal of Social Work*, 45 (1): 52–68.

Maslach, C. (1976) 'Burned out', *Human Behaviour*, 5: 16–22.

Masten, A.S. (2001) 'Ordinary magic: Resilience processes in development', *American Psychologist*, 56: 227–38.

Mayer, J.D. and Faber, M.A. (2010) 'Personal intelligence and resilience', in J.W. Reich, A.J. Zautra and J.S. Hall (eds), *Handbook of Adult Resilience*. New York: Guilford Press.

McGregor, D. (1960) *The Human Side of Enterprise*. New York: McGraw Hill.

McGregor, K. (2012a) 'Nine out of 10 social workers believe hotdesking saps morale', *Community Care*, 6 November 2012. Available at: www.communitycare.co.uk/2012/11/06/nine-out-of-10-social-workers-believe-hotdesking-saps-morale/

McGregor, K. (2012b) 'Government cuts have left social workers "drowning in admin"', *Community Care*, 17 May 2012. Available at: www.communitycare.co.uk/2012/05/17/government-cuts-hare-left-social-workers-drawing-in-admin

McGregor, K. (2013) 'Third of UK's social workers not currently receiving supervision', *Community Care*. Available at: www.communitycare.co.uk/2013/06/18/third-of-uks-social-workers-not-currently-receiving-supervision/

Miller, M.D. and Harrington, K.M. (2011) 'Personality factors in resilience factors in resilience to traumatic stress', in S.M. Southwick, B.T. Litz, D. Charney and M.J. Friedman (eds), *Resilience and Mental Health: Challenges across the lifespan*. New York: Cambridge University Press.

Moffitt, P. (2009) 'Mindfulness and compassion: Tools for transforming suffering into joy', in Barry Boyce (ed.), *In the Face of Fear: Buddhist wisdom for challenging times*. Boston, MA: Shambhala Publications.

Molden, D. and Hutchinson, P. (2008) *How to Be Confident Using the Power of NLP*. Edinburgh: Pearson Education Ltd.

Morgan, H. and Thomas, K. (1996) 'A psychodynamic perspective on group processes', in Margaret Wetherall (ed.), *Identities, Groups and Social Issues*. Milton Keynes: Open University Press.

Morrison, T. (2005) *Staff Supervision in Social Care*. Harlow: Longman.

Munro, E. (2011) *Munro Review of Child Protection Final Report: A child-centred system.* Department for Education. Available at: www.gov.uk/government/uploads/system/uploads/attachment_data/file/175391/Munro-Review.pdf

National Council for Voluntary Organisations (2013) Counting the Cuts: The impact of spending cuts on the UK voluntary and community sectors – 2013 update. Available at: www.ncvo.org.uk/images/documents/policy_and_research/funding/counting_the_cuts_2013.pdf

Neenan, M. (2009) *Developing Resilience: A cognitive-behavioural approach.* London: Routledge.

Noble, C. and Irwin, J. (2009) 'An exploration of the current challenges in a rapidly changing social, economic and political environment', *Journal of Social Work*, 9 (3): 345–58.

Nourbakhsh, I.R. (2015) 'The coming robot dystopia: all too inhuman', *Foreign Affairs*, July–August 2015: 23–8.

O'Connor, S. and O'Murchu, C. (2011) 'Britain's private care homes face crisis', *Financial Times*, 30 May 2011. Available at: http://www.ft.com/cms/s/0/307bbd3e-8af5-11e0-b2f1-00144feab49a.html#axzz3hUG4JWdk

Office of National Statistics (2015) Statistical Bulletin: Personal Well-being in the UK 2014 to 2015. Available at: www.ons.gov.uk/peoplepopulationandcommunity/wellbeing/bulletins/measuringnationalwellbeing/2015-09-23

Otomo, K. (1991) *Roujin Z* (animated film). London: Manga Entertainment.

Oxfordshire Safeguarding Children Board (2015) *Serious Case Review into Child Sexual Exploitation in Oxfordshire: From the experiences of Children A, B, C, D, E, and F.* Available at: http://www.oscb.org.uk/wp-content/uploads/SCR-into-CSE-in-Oxfordshire-FINAL-FOR-WEBSITE.pdf

Pargament, K.I. and Cummings, J. (2010) 'Anchored by faith: "Religion as a resilience factor"', in J.W. Reich, A.J. Zautra and J.S. Hall (eds), *Handbook of Adult Resilience.* New York: The Guilford Press.

Petty, M.M. and Odewahn, C.A. (1983) 'Supervisory behaviour and sex role stereotypes in human services organisations'. *Clinical Supervisor*, 1 (2): 13–20.

Pine, B.A. and Healy, L.M. (2007) 'New leadership for the human services: Involving and empowering staff through participatory management', in J. Aldgate, L. Healy, B. Malcolm, B. Pine, W. Rose and J. Seden (eds) *Enhancing Social Work Management: Theory and best practice from the UK and USA.* London: Jessica Kingsley.

Pines, A. and Aronson, E. with Kafry, D. (1981) *Burnout: From tedium to personal growth.* New York: Free Press.

Pines, A. and Maslach, C. (1978) 'Characteristics of staff burnout in mental health settings', *Hospital and Community Psychiatry*, 29: 233–7.

Purrington, C., Butler, C. and Gale, S.F. (2003) *Built to Learn: The inside story of how Rockwell Collins became a learning organisation.* New York: AMACOM.

Ricard, M. (2009) 'Optimism, pessimism and naivete,' in Barry Boyce (ed.), *In the Face of Fear: Buddhist wisdom for challenging times.* Boston, MA: Shambhala Publications.

Richardson, G.E. (2002) 'The metatheory of resilience and resiliency', *Journal of Clinical Psychology*, 58: 307–21.

Robinson, D. (1997) *Too Nice for Your Own Good: How to stop making 9 self-sabotaging mistakes.* New York: Warner Books.

Robinson, J.B. (1990) 'Futures under glass: A recipe for people who hate to predict', *Futures*, 22 (8): 820–42.

Rogers, C. (1959) 'A theory of therapy, personality and interpersonal relationships as developed in the client-centered framework', in S. Koch (ed.), *Psychology: A study of a science. Vol. 3: Formulations of the person and the social context.* New York: McGraw Hill.

Rosen, L. (2015) 'Take a break', *Harvard Business Review*, June 2015.

Rotter, J.B. (1966) 'Generalized expectancies for internal versus external control of reinforcement', *Psychological Monographs: General & Applied*, 80 (1): 1–28.

Rutter, M. (1987) 'Psychological resilience and protective mechanisms', *American Journal of Orthopsychiatry*, 57: 316–31.

Schrieber, P. (1987) 'The wit and wisdom of Grace Hopper', *COCLC Newsletter 167*, March/April 1987.

Schön, D. (2002) *From Technical Rationality to Reflection-in-action*. San Francisco: Jossey-Bass.

Schraer, R. (2015) 'Social worker hauled before the regulator for "trolling" David Cameron', *Community Care* website, 30 January 2015. Available at: www.communitycare.co.uk/2015/01/30/social-worker-hauled-regulator-trolling-david-cameron

Schulte, M.J., Ree, M.J. and Carretta, T.R. (2004) 'Emotional intelligence: Not much more than g and personality', *Personality and Individual Differences*, 37: 1059–68.

Seligman, M.E.P. (1975) *Helplessness: On depression, development and death*. San Francisco: W.H. Freeman.

Selye, H. (1956) *The Stress of Life*. New York: McGraw-Hill.

Shonin, E., van Gordon, W. and Griffiths, M.D. (2015) 'Mindfulness – A breath of fresh air?', *The Psychologist*, 28 (1): 28–31.

Skills for Care (2014) *Critically Reflective Action Learning*. Leeds: Skills for Care. Available at: http://www.skillsforcare.org.uk/Document-library/Social-work/Action-Learning/Critical-reflective-action-learning.pdf

Skodol, A.E. (2010) 'The resilient personality', in J.W. Reich, A.J. Zautra and J.S. Hall (eds) *Handbook of Adult Resilience*. New York: Guilford Press.

Smith, R. (2012) '"ICS is the bane of my life" says child protection social worker', *Community Care*, 2 November 2012. Available at: www.communitycare.co.uk/blogs/social-work-blog/2012/11/ics-is-the-bane-of-my-life/

Social Care Workforce Research Unit (2014) *Evaluation of the Social Work Practices with Adults Pilots*. London: King's College London. Available at: https://www.kcl.ac.uk/sspp/policy-institute/scwru/pubs/2014/reports/Social-Work-Practices-w-Adults-FINAL-EVALUATION-REPORT-2014.pdf

Southwick, S.M., Litz, B.T., Charney, D. and Friedman, M.J. (2011) *Resilience and Mental Health: Challenges across the lifespan*. New York: Cambridge University Press.

Spreitzer, G. and Porath, C. (2012) 'Creating sustainable performance', *Harvard Business Review*, January–February 2012.

Staats, B.R. and Upton, D.M. (2011) 'Lean knowledge work', *Harvard Business Review*. October 2011.

Stein, S.J. and Book H.E. (2006) *The EQ Edge: Emotional intelligence and your success*. Mississauga, ON: Jossey Bass.

Stogdill, R. (1974) *Handbook of Leadership: A survey of theory and research*. New York: Free Press.

Tham, P. and Meagher, G. (2009) 'Working in human services: How do experiences and working conditions in child welfare social work compare?', *British Journal of Social Work*, 29 (5): 807–27.

Tummers, L., Steijn, B. and Bekkers, V. (2013) 'Public professionals and policy alienation', in M. Noordegraaf and B. Steijn (eds), *Professionals Under Pressure: The reconfiguration of professional work in changing public services*. Amsterdam University Press.

Van Heugten, K. (2004) 'Co-worker violence toward social workers: Too hard to handle?', *Social Work Review*, 16 (4): 66–73.

Van Heugten, K. (2011) *Social Work Under Pressure: How to overcome stress, fatigue and burnout in the workplace.* London: Jessica Kingsley.

Vargus, I.D. (1980) 'The minority administrator', in S.Salvin and F.D. Perlmutter (eds), *Leadership in Social Administration.* Philadelphia: Temple University Press.

Wallop, H. (2014) 'Are you getting enough sleep?', *The Telegraph,* 14 May 2014.

Weeks, H. (2001) 'Taking the stress out of stressful conversations', *Harvard Business Review,* July–August 2001.

Weinbach, R.W. and Taylor, L.M. (2011) *The Social Worker as Manager.* Boston, MA: Allyn and Bacon.

Wilson, K., Ruch, G., Lymbery, M. and Cooper, A. (2008) *Social Work: An introduction to contemporary practice.* Harlow: Pearson Education.

Winter, E. (2015) 'Stockholm Bias: It's not quite Stockholm Syndrome but it affects all of us', *Forbes Magazine* website, 8 April 2015. Available at: http://www.forbes.com/sites/forbesleadershipfo rum/2015/04/08/stockholm-bias-its-not-quite-stockholm-syndrome-but-it-affects-all-of-us/

Wiseman, L. and McKeown, G. (2010) 'Bringing out the best in your people', *Harvard Business Review,* May 2010.

Wonnacott, J. (2012) *Mastering Social Work Supervision.* London: Jessica Kingsley.

Zaccaro, S.J., Kemp, C. and Bader, P. (2004) *Leader Traits and Attributes. The nature of leadership.* Thousand Oaks, CA: Sage.

Zautra. A.J., Hall, J.S. and Murray, K.E. (2010) 'Resilience: A new definition of health for people and communities', in J.W. Reich, A.J. Zautra and J.S. Hall (eds), *Handbook of Adult Resilience.* New York: The Guilford Press.

INDEX